D0129335

TRAINING DESIGN *Basics*

SAUL CARLINER

A Complete, How-to Guide to Help You:

- Create Quality, Performance-Based Training

- Develop Fundamental Training Design Skills

- Ensure Your Training Program Meets Learner Needs

ASTD
Linking People,
Learning & Performance

ASTD Press is an internationally renowned source of insightful and practical information on workplace learning and performance topics, including training basics, evaluation and return-on-investment (ROI), instructional systems development (ISD), e-learning, leadership, and career development.

Ordering information: Books published by ASTD Press can be purchased by visiting our Website at store.astd.org or by calling 800.628.2783 or 703.683.8100.

Library of Congress Control Number: 2003112227

ISBN-10: 1-56286-348-7
ISBN-13: 978-1-56286-348-7

Acquisitions and Development Editor: Mark Morrow
Copyeditor: Karen Eddleman
Interior Design and Production: Kathleen Schaner
Cover Design: Ana Ilieva
Cover Illustration: Phil and Jim Bliss

Printed by Victor Graphics, Inc. Baltimore, MD
www.victorgraphics.com

Table of Contents

■ ■

About the *Training Basics* Series vii

Preface ix

1. **The Basics of Training Design** 1
   What Is Design for Training? 1
   Basic Principles of Training Design 2
   Three Essentials of Human Performance Improvement 2
   Seven Must-Follow Principles of Adult Learning 5
   The Basic Process—The ADDIE Approach to Instructional Design 8
   Getting It Done 13

2. **The Basics of Planning a Training Project** 17
   Who Works on a Training Project? 18
   Assumptions About Your Project 24
   When Will You Finish the Program? 26
   How Much Is the Program Going to Cost? 34
   Getting It Done 36

3. **The Basic Information Needed to Start a Project** 43
   Six Basic Needs Analysis Steps 43
   Four Methods of Uncovering Needs 56
   One More Thing 60
   Getting It Done 60

4. The Basic Instructional Objective **65**

The Basic Value of Objectives and Evaluation 66

The Basics of Setting Objectives 66

Writing Objectives...68

Distinguishing Among Main and Supporting Objectives 70

Drafting the Evaluation 70

Basic Issues of Evaluation 72

Getting It Done 78

5. The Basics of Organizing Courses **83**

Beginning the Design Process 84

Media for Communicating Learning Content 84

The Basics of Organizing Content 88

Getting It Done 95

6. The Basic Strategies for Presenting Content..............................**99**

Characteristics of an Engaging Course..100

Five Basic Strategies for Communicating Learning Content 101

Beginning and Ending Courses...110

Choosing an Instructional Strategy 113

Getting It Done 115

7. The Basics of Developing Course Materials **117**

Getting Started..117

The Basics of Preparing Materials for the Classroom 118

The Basics of Preparing Workbook-Based Courses.......................132

Getting It Done 134

8. The Basics of Producing Learning Materials **139**

Getting Started..139

Techniques for Communicating Learning Content.......................140

Basic Rules for Preparing Visuals 144

The Basics of Preparing Workbooks 150

The Basics of the Production Process 155

Getting It Done...158

9. The Basic Quality Checks for a New Course..........................**161**

    What Is Formative Evaluation? 162

    The Three Basic Types of Formative Evaluation.........................163

    The Basics of Revision..169

    Getting It Done..174

10. The Basics of Administering Your Course **177**

    The Basics of Administering Courses...178

    The Basics of Marketing Courses..185

    The Basics of Supporting Training Programs 189

    Closing a Design and Development Project................................192

    Getting It Done..195

References...197

Additional Resources 199

About the Author 203

About the
Training Basics Series

■■■

ASTD's *Training Basics* series recognizes and, in some ways, celebrates the fast-paced, ever-changing reality of organizations today. Jobs, roles, and expectations change quickly. One day you might be a network administrator or a process line manager, and the next day you might be asked to train 50 employees in basic computer skills or to instruct line workers in quality processes.

Where do you turn for help? The ASTD *Training Basics* series is designed to be your one-stop solution. The series takes a minimalist approach to your learning curve dilemma and presents only the information you need to be successful. Each book in the series guides you through key aspects of training: giving presentations, making the transition to the role of trainer, designing and delivering training, and evaluating training. The books in the series also include some advanced skills such as performance and basic business proficiencies.

The ASTD *Training Basics* series is the perfect tool for training and performance professionals looking for easy-to-understand materials that will prepare non-trainers to take on a training role. In addition, this series is the perfect reference tool for any trainer's bookshelf and a quick way to hone your existing skills. The titles currently planned in the series include:

- ▶ *Presentation Basics*
- ▶ *Trainer Basics*
- ▶ *Training Design Basics*
- ▶ *Facilitation Basics*
- ▶ *Job Aid Basics*
- ▶ *ROI Basics*
- ▶ *Needs Assessment Basics*
- ▶ *Evaluation Basics*
- ▶ *Organization Development Basics*
- ▶ *Performance Basics*

- ▶ *Coaching Basics*
- ▶ *Communication Basics*

Preface

■■

Training Design Basics explains how to design and develop training programs, primarily those programs intended for the classroom or taught through workbooks.

It focuses on designing and developing these programs in the *real* world. In that world, trainers must make do with the time and resources available. Yes, trainers have to analyze needs and write objectives. After all, trainers must know what they are training and why they are doing so before they develop a training program. But, often the time to get this information is limited, so this book suggests ways to get the information even if the course designer and developer doesn't have the time or access to all of the people who might be helpful.

In addition, many design books concentrate on the analysis phases of the design process. In contrast, this one gives as much attention to the design and development phases, exploring how to structure a course (including the parts of every course that would not appear in an outline), strategies for presenting content, identifying the materials that you need to develop (such as student and instructor guides), and suggesting design and communication tips to follow when developing the materials.

Similarly, although e-learning and other forms of instruction receive much attention, the bulk of training still takes place in the classroom. Therefore, the emphasis here is on preparing classroom courses.

Finally, after designing and developing training programs, most trainers have responsibility for launching and running these programs. These issues are explored, too, especially as they relate to administering, marketing, and supporting courses so that they are likely to be effective.

Who Should Read This Book?

Training Design Basics is aimed toward new course designers and developers, and instructors who are primarily concerned with developing courses for the classroom or workbooks (but not for e-learning). Additionally, subject matter experts (SMEs) can benefit from this book as they find themselves thrust into training roles. Other nontrainers who find themselves responsible for designing and developing classroom courses and training workbooks will be able to put the guidance offered here to effective use.

How *Training Design Basics* Is Organized

This book consists of 10 chapters. They cover:

1. "The Basics of Training Design" offers an overview of the issues you need to consider when designing courses, including the concepts of human performance improvement and adult learning.

2. "The Basics of Planning a Training Project" provides an overview of the design process and suggests ways to answer the question, "How much time is needed to design and develop a course," even before you start development. This chapter also describes the roles that people play on a training project and suggests ways for effectively working with clients.

3. "The Basic Information Needed to Start a Project" identifies the information you need to make effective design decisions, why you need that information, and offers suggestions on how to get that information when you have a tight schedule.

4. "The Basic Instructional Objective" explains how to concretely state the goals of a course and how to assess whether learners have achieved those goals (a step you perform before beginning to design courses).

5. "The Basics of Organizing Courses" explains the general structure of a course, and how to divide content into units.

6. "The Basic Strategies for Presenting Content" explores a variety of ways to present content so that it engages learners and they retain the material.

7. "The Basics of Developing Course Materials" identifies the types of materials you must develop for courses, including student materials, visuals (such as slides or transparencies), and instructor notes for classroom and workbook-based courses.

8. "The Basics of Producing Learning Materials" describes guidelines for writing and designing student and instructor materials, as well as considerations for producing them.

9. "The Basic Quality Checks for a New Course" explains how to conduct reviews and pilot classes to ensure the accuracy and effectiveness of the materials.
10. "The Basics of Administering Your Course" makes clear the responsibilities of course designers and developers after a course "goes public."

This book strives to make it as easy as possible for you to understand and apply its lessons. Icons throughout the book help you identify key points that can mean the difference between a successful presentation and an embarrassing one.

What's Inside This Chapter

Each chapter opens with a short list—really a quick access guide—to introduce you to the rest of the chapter. If you are reading this book, you're probably in a hurry to get something done. You can use this section to identify the information it contains and, if you wish, skip ahead to the material that will be most useful to you.

Think About This

These little helpful reminders are like extra tools in your designer's toolkit. Think of them as an extra layer of preparation of knowledge to build your confidence.

Basic Rules

These rules cut to the chase. Although they are easy to remember, they are extremely important concepts for every designer.

Noted

Sometimes a point or suggested practice needs some additional detail to help you understand the concept. Or, perhaps a little digression would be helpful to make a point. You will find these items under the "noted" icon.

Getting It Done

The final section of each chapter offers you a chance to practice some of the concepts discussed in the chapter and provides final tips and pointers to help you apply what you have learned.

Acknowledgments

This book represents a collaboration among many people. I thank course developers Jeff Bell, Lynn Harris, and Ron Wincek for serving as my sanity checks and for sharing their expertise as course designers and developers. I also acknowledge the staff of the Seattle's Best Coffee café in Pikesville, Maryland, for giving me a comfortable place to work and my family members for their support as I wrote it. Finally, thanks to Mark Morrow, Karen Eddleman, and Kathleen Schaner—the editorial team at ASTD—for great advice and production assistance.

Saul Carliner
October 2003

1

The Basics
of Training Design

▪▪▪

What's Inside This Chapter

This chapter introduces you to the concept of design for training. Specifically it addresses the following:

▶ What is "design" for training?
▶ The basic principles that guide course designers: human performance improvement and the seven must-follow principles of adult learning
▶ The basic process that course designers follow, called ADDIE.

In addition, a checklist at the end of this chapter identifies issues you should keep in mind as you approach a design and development project.

What Is Design for Training?

Before the handouts get placed on the seats, before the initial "Good morning," before the opening exercise, and before the first teaching sequence, trainers invest substantial effort in planning a course—as much as 40 hours of preparatory work for each hour of classroom instruction.

1

Most trainers feel that this up-front effort is essential to the success of their work. The more they learn about a training problem in advance, the better that trainers can target the instruction to address that need, reduce the risk of the unknown in the classroom, and help learners master the new skills.

The framework for analyzing a training problem, defining the intended outcomes, determining how to present the content to learners to achieve those outcomes, developing the training course according to the designs, implementing the course, and evaluating its effectiveness is called the *instructional design process*. Trainers use instructional design to prepare all types of instruction—courses presented in the classroom, through workbooks, and online.

Although many associate design with the arts, the true purpose of design is problem solving. Good instruction addresses problems because education results in a change in behavior. Sometimes that change affects physical behavior (called *psychomotor skills*), such as following a new process for changing tires on a car. Sometimes that change affects intellectual behavior (called *cognitive skills*), such as following a new methodology for determining credit worthiness. Sometimes that change in behavior affects attitudes (called *affective skills*), such as changing attitudes toward smoking. Therefore, one of the key elements of the design process is determining which behaviors need to be changed, the skills and knowledge that learners must develop to master the desired behavior, and the motivators that would encourage or discourage learners from adopting those behaviors on the job.

Basic Principles of Training Design

In addition to being guided by a thorough understanding of the problem, design is also guided by certain general principles:

- ▸ the principles that constitute the field of *human performance improvement*, which help to ensure that people achieve the best possible results on the job
- ▸ the principles that underpin adult learning.

The next two sections explore these two sets of principles.

Three Essentials of Human Performance Improvement

More than preparing courses that teach people to do something, training professionals are in the business of improving human performance. That is, the primary job of trainers is working with the leaders of organizations to help make workers more measurably effective in their work. Effectiveness is usually measured in specific ways, such as the number of widgets produced per hour, the number of calls handled per hour, the number of products sold, or the number of errors.

Basic Rule 1

Not all performance problems can be solved through training. The principles of promoting effective work are called the principles of *human performance improvement* (HPI). (You might also hear people call it *human performance technology*.) The principles of HPI play a profound role in the design of training programs.

1. All Training Programs Must Produce Measurable Improvements in Human Behavior

If the purpose of training is to help make workers measurably more effective in their work, then training professionals must specifically identify the behaviors that should improve and how to measure those behaviors before work begins on the training program. After workers complete the training program, training professionals should follow the performance of learners on the job and measure changes in that on-the-job behavior.

Furthermore, these improvements in behavior must offer tangible benefits to the organization sponsoring the training. Ideally, these tangible benefits are financial. For example, if workers produce more widgets per hour, organizations have more widgets to sell. Or, if learners reduce the number of errors in their work, organizations reduce the cost of doing work over, called *rework*. But sometimes, these benefits are intangible, such as more empathetic customer service. Such changes often lead to financial rewards, too. For example, better customer service can result in improved retention of customers.

2. Training Programs Must Address the Gap Between Current and Ideal Performance

This gap is called the *performance gap*. Although the gap itself is usually self-evident, the reasons that it exists usually are not. The cause of the gap is best uncovered through an analysis of the situation.

For example, if the number one complaint against customer service representatives is that they appeared to be rude (as recorded in the call log), the performance gap is the difference between behavior perceived as rude and that perceived as polite. To find the cause of the behavior, you might talk to customers who complained to find out what they thought was rude, to the supervisors who handled the complaints to see how serious the problem was, and to the workers to find out why they handled calls in the way that they did.

3. Training Might Not Fill the Performance Gap

Taking a training class alone does not always result in measurable changes in workplace behavior. This happens because training only addresses one of the three drivers of performance: skills and knowledge. In some instances, workers *do* have the skills and knowledge to handle a task, but still do not perform the task effectively. In such situations, some other factor affects performance. That factor might be:

> ▶ *a lack of tools or resources needed to perform the task:* For example, suppose workers receive training on new word-processing software, but the software has not yet been installed on their PCs. The workers cannot perform the skills learned in the training course because they do not have the software resources on which to practice the skills.
>
> ▶ *motivation:* Even if workers have the skills, knowledge, and resources to do their jobs, a lack of motivation can affect performance. Consider again the example of rude customer service representatives. Complaints lodged against them might simply result from the customer service representatives lacking skills in handling belligerent customers. Or, strict time limits on calls might be the problem. When customer service representatives exceed that time limit, they are reprimanded. So, the representatives abruptly end calls with customers to avoid being reprimanded by their supervisors. Solving this problem requires removing the limit on the length of calls, not training in polite customer service behavior.

Because some solutions for closing the performance gap do not require training courses, solutions are called *interventions.* Using this term helps training professionals keep an open mind about the approach they take. If the performance gap results from a lack of skills and knowledge, training professionals recommend a training course. If it results from a lack of resources or motivation, training professionals recommend different types of interventions, ones more likely to address those issues.

This book explains how to design training courses and exclusively focuses on those performance gaps resulting from a lack of skills and knowledge. Despite that singular focus, please keep in mind that the solutions to the problems you encounter in your work environment might require other types of interventions.

Basic Rule 2

When designing and presenting training courses, treat adult learners like adults. Adults approach learning differently than children do. Adults enter training with experience, with preconceived notions of the subject, and with other needs.

Seven Must-Follow Principles of Adult Learning

1. Adult Learning Is Andragogy, Not Pedagogy

Andragogy, a term popularized by Malcolm Knowles (1988), refers to the art and science of teaching adults. Andragogy encompasses principles that instructional designers must address when preparing learning programs for adults. Pedagogy, on the other hand, refers to the art and science of teaching children, whose learning needs differ significantly from those of adults.

2. Adult Learners Are Pressed for Time

Adults squeeze in learning between demanding jobs, family responsibilities, and community commitments. Even when highly motivated to learn, the call of life limits the time that many adults can invest in learning.

3. Adult Learners Are Goal Oriented

Adults primarily participate in learning programs to achieve a particular goal. The goal may be work related, such as using a computer system more effectively or writing a performance plan that conforms to company guidelines. The learning goal might be personal, such as the desire to learn basic Japanese in advance of a vacation in Japan or learning Adobe PhotoShop to prepare a family Website. Classroom trainers often begin courses by asking how learners hope to benefit from a course and many tailor their content accordingly.

4. Adult Learners Bring Previous Knowledge and Experience

Whenever possible, linking new material in a course to learners' existing knowledge and experience creates a powerful and relevant learning experience. In some instances, however, content in the training program contradicts material that people previously learned. In such situations, designers of training programs must first convince learners to part with the old approach so they can grasp the new.

In other situations, learners already know some or all of the content covered in a training course. Many time-pressed adult learners prefer not to review known content again. To avoid such unnecessary duplication, designers of training programs need to carefully assess what learners already know and let them skip familiar material.

5. Adult Learners Have a Finite Capacity for Information

Although many training courses tackle complex topics, most learners are primarily interested in aspects of the content that directly affect them. In many cases, that's just a small part of the content.

In contrast, because they have so little time with learners, many trainers want to cram in as much content as they can. Because learners see limited application of the additional content, they absorb little of it, sometimes tuning out the content that directly affects them. In the classroom, instructors usually detect this situation when eyes glaze over with an "I'm overwhelmed" look.

6. Adult Learners Have Different Motivation Levels

During the first six weeks to three months on a job, adults are highly motivated to learn. When faced with a new work process or approach, adults are similarly motivated to learn. (What stifles their motivation, at this point, is fear of failure and difficulty of unlearning old habits.) As they become more familiar with the content, learners' motivation to learn wanes until a specific need arises. The challenge to designers of training programs is identifying the motivation level of learners as their expertise grows, and matching content to that level of motivation.

Think About This

When designing training courses, designers tailor the content and teaching style to the motivation level of the learner. Most people go through three phases of motivation (Carliner, 2002):

- *Novice stage:* During this stage, the learner's primary learning goal is getting started—learning enough material to proficiently handle the routine tasks. Learners only need how-to instruction and supervision at this point. Don't overburden students with too much content or overwhelm them with unnecessary choices. (That is, although five ways to complete a task might exist, just teach the easiest one at this point.)
- *Feeling arrogant stage:* Learners have mastered routine tasks and gained confidence. Now they want to learn how to handle routine tasks more efficiently and how to handle some less common tasks. Learners still want instruction at this point, but some do not want supervision or practice. So just tell learners what to do; let them choose whether or not they want to practice.
- *Feeling humble stage:* At this stage, most learners are aware of the limits of their knowledge. Learning usually happens informally, one expert to another. In situations like these, learners appreciate discussion groups and other, less formal learning programs in which they can research answers to their specific questions.

7. Adult Learners Have Different Learning Styles

Learning style refers to the way in which a person prefers to pick up new content. Each person has a number of preferred learning styles.

Learning Versus Doing. Some people prefer doing tasks with minimal briefing. That is, they prefer to pick up content through trial and error, with little supervision. Then—through a debriefing process—they put labels on the ideas covered in the trial-and-error activity and learn how to apply those concepts more broadly. This is called the *do-then-learn* style.

In contrast, other people prefer to learn everything first, then perform a task, reducing the likelihood of errors when trying something for the first time. This is called the *learn-then-do* style.

Verbal Versus Hands-on. Another set of learning styles pertains to the sense through which a person most easily acquires new knowledge. Some learners are verbal learners; they learn best by reading. Other learners are visual learners; they learn best by seeing pictures. Auditory learners learn best by hearing, and kinesthetic learners learn best by touch (hands-on experience).

Designing for Different Learning Styles. In an ideal world, each learning program would be able to accommodate the different learning styles of all the learners. Learners would more likely master the content because they learn in their preferred style.

Practical reality requires that course designers would have to design and develop separate versions of each training program to accommodate each learning style (for example, a visual version of a training program as well as a verbal version). Because that's not usually feasible, designers try to account for the variety of learning styles by using many different strategies to present content throughout a training program.

For example, one section of a course might be more visual than verbal to accommodate visual learners. Another might start with a hands-on exercise to accommodate learners who prefer to learn through discovery.

The Basic Process—The ADDIE Approach to Instructional Design

With the principles of HPI and androgogy guiding them, training professionals design training courses. When designing a training course, course designers and developers follow a structured process. Its generic name is ADDIE for each of the five phases of the process: analysis, design, development, implementation, and evaluation.

Analysis

Analysis encompasses the activities required to understand the training problem and define the objectives that the training course should achieve. Specifically, analysis involves a set of activities that are explained in the following sections.

Researching the Problem. These activities include identifying the business goal to be achieved through the training program and the performance gap that the program must address. When identifying the performance gap, training professionals identify what excellent performance looks like, as well as the tasks and skills that learners must master to reach excellent performance.

Basic Rule 3

Effective training requires not only a thorough understanding of the training problem, but also a well-stated definition of the results to be achieved and a well-thought-out plan for achieving those results. Therefore, training professionals prefer to take a methodical approach to designing courses. This methodical approach breaks down the task of designing courses into manageable steps and ensures that training professionals attend to each of the myriad details in the design process.

The approach dates back to World War II, when the U.S. military was introducing sophisticated new equipment into the battlefield and needed effective training designed quickly. Although this model has been improved upon over the years, the original version of instructional systems design (ISD) essentially remains the same today, with the five key categories of activities summed up in ADDIE.

This research also includes information about the learners—who they are, what they already know, how they feel about their jobs, and the challenges they might experience as they work toward new levels of performance.

Last, the research includes information about the learning and working environments. These factors might affect learners' ability to learn and apply the knowledge back on the job. Analysis must also identify constraints affecting the project, such as the drop-dead date when the project is due, the not-to-exceed budget (the maximum the organization sponsoring the training course is willing to invest), and other environmental issues that affect the design and development of the training program. Chapter 3 identifies in more detail the information you need to start a training project.

Defining the Objectives of the Training Program. This step involves stating the tasks that learners must achieve to successfully bridge the performance gap in observable and measurable terms. Training professionals use a specific language to write objectives so that they can effectively assess whether the objectives have been achieved. Chapter 4 explains in more detail how to write objectives so you can effectively assess whether they have been achieved.

Preparing the Assessment of Learning. Also known as the test of learning, this assessment represents what successful learning looks like, so you prepare it before beginning any work on the design of the training course. In this way, you "teach to the test" to ensure that highest number of learners master the content. Test questions emerge directly from the objectives.

Because the objectives identify the goals of the learning program, teaching to the test is desirable in training because it ensures that training is focused on the goals and does not veer off into irrelevant content. Chapter 4 explains how to write tests.

Design

In the final last activities of analysis, you determined which content to cover in the training course. Through design activities, you determine how to present that content. Specifically, design involves:

▶ *Choosing the appropriate intervention for achieving the objectives:* Although this book assumes that training is the appropriate solution to the problem, in the real world, this assumption is not valid. If the performance gap results from a lack of resources or motivation, the intervention should address those issues because training will not solve the problem. This book focuses on training so it does not explore other possible interventions.

▶ *Structuring the content for the course:* Structuring the content first involves understanding the medium used to communicate the training content, such as the classroom, the computer, or a workbook. Different media have different characteristics. Although research has shown that each medium is equally effective in teaching, research and practical experience have also shown that what makes effective teaching differs in each medium. For example, classroom learners need a break every 60 to 90 minutes; workbook learners need breaks more frequently than that.

Then, structuring involves sequencing the material in the course, and in each unit. In doing so, you consider the general structure of each unit so that units all have a similar rhythm, divide all of the content into manageable units, consider how to help slower learners master the content, and how to enrich the material for highly motivated learners. Chapter 5 explains how to structure the content.

▶ *Presenting the content:* After determining the structure of the content, you next determine how to present it. You choose among a variety of instructional techniques, such as the classical approach, mastery learning, and discovery learning. Chapter 6 describes the different techniques available.

Development

Development is the phase when you convert your design plans into course materials. For classroom courses, you develop slides, lecture notes, and handouts for the course. You also develop the instructor's materials for administering learning activities; you may need to create databases and other materials for computer exercises, answer keys for question-and-answer exercises, and discussion guides for class discussions. For workbooks, you develop the workbook and related materials, such as visuals.

Chapter 7 identifies the types of materials you must develop for courses. Chapter 8 describes guidelines for writing and designing these materials and suggests some considerations for producing them.

In addition, during the development phase you have technical professionals review the content to make sure it is accurate. You also run a pilot of the course with people who represent the intended learners to find out which parts of the course work well and which parts need improvement. Finally, you check for editorial issues, such as consistency in terminology and appropriate use of headings. Chapter 9 describes issues to consider as you plan for technical and editorial reviews.

Implementation

After the materials are printed, you are ready for learners to take the course. This process is called *implementation,* and it involves more than distributing workbooks and teaching classes. Implementation also involves ongoing classroom support, such as scheduling class sessions, instructors, classrooms, and equipment (both audiovisual and lab equipment), and making sure that the learning materials arrive at the classroom on time.

Implementation also involves marketing the course—promoting the course on an ongoing basis to the intended learners. Usually, marketing is handled by publishing a course catalog and regularly sending out targeted email messages and flyers by surface mail to keep awareness high.

Finally, implementation means maintaining the course. This involves making changes to content and resources found to be in error and updating the content as changes to business processes, technology, and other issues require.

In many instances, the person who handles these tasks differs from the person who originally designs and develops the course. Nevertheless, the person who develops the course needs to be aware of these issues and must plan for them. Chapter 10 explores implementation issues.

Evaluation

Evaluation is the ultimate phase in the process of designing a training course. Evaluation is an activity that is intended to assess whether the courses have achieved their objectives.

Evaluation occurs on a number of different levels, following a model first proposed in 1959 by Donald Kirkpatrick (1998). The four levels of evaluation in the Kirkpatrick model are shown in table 1-1.

This book only addresses levels 1, 2, and 3 of evaluation. Chapter 4 provides some information about what's involved in these levels and presents a sample of a satisfaction survey (level 1) and describes how to develop a criterion-referenced test (level 2). Other books in ASTD's *Training Basics* series explain in more detail how to conduct course evaluations.

Table 1-1. Kirkpatrick's (1998) four levels of evaluation.

Level	Name	Issues Assessed at This Level
1	Reaction	Assesses learners' initial reactions to a course. Their reactions, in turn, offer insights into learners' satisfaction with a course. Trainers usually assess this level through a survey, often called a "smiley sheet." Occasionally, trainers use focus groups and similar methods to receive more specific comments (called *qualitative feedback*) on the courses.
2	Learning	Assesses the extent to which learners achieved the objectives. Trainers usually assess this with a criterion-referenced test. The criteria are the course objectives. The tests usually involve answering questions or participating in a demonstration observed by an instructor.
3	Transfer	Assesses the extent to which learners actually apply the lessons learned in a course in everyday work six weeks to six months after taking the course (perhaps longer). This assessment is based on the objectives of the course and carried out through tests, observations, surveys, and interviews with co-workers and supervisors.
4	Business results	Assesses the impact of the training course on the bottom line of the organization six months to two years after the course (the actual time varies depending on the context of the course). For many reasons, this is the most difficult level to measure. First, most training courses do not have explicitly written business objectives, such as "this course should reduce support expenses by 20 percent." Second, the methodology for assessing business impact is not yet refined. Some assess this measurement by tracking business measurements, others assess through observations, some by surveys, and still others assess by qualitative measures. Last, after six months or more, evaluators have difficulty attributing changed business results solely to training when changes in personnel, systems, and other factors might also have contributed to changes in business performance.

Getting It Done

As you begin a training project, you need to build upon a few fundamentals, which will continually arise as you face specific design challenges. Exercise 1-1 helps reinforce your learning about the basics presented in this chapter.

Exercise 1-1. Reinforcing the Basics of Design.

Fill in the blanks.

1. Design is:

    _____

    _____

    _____

2. Two basic sets of principles that guide trainers are:

    _____ and _____.

3. Human performance improvement refers to:

    _____

    _____

    _____

4. Nearly all training is intended for adults, who approach learning differently than children. Name at least three of the seven principles of adult learning described in this book.

    _____

    _____

    _____

5. Trainers follow a methodical approach to designing training courses called ADDIE. What does ADDIE stand for?

    A   _____

    D   _____

    D   _____

    I   _____

    E   _____

(continued on page 14)

> ## Exercise 1-1. Reinforcing the Basics of Design (continued).

Answers

1. Design is a problem-solving activity and, in terms of training, refers to the framework for analyzing a training problem, defining the intended outcomes, determining how to present the content to learners to achieve those outcomes, developing the training course according to the designs, implementing the course, and evaluating its effectiveness.

2. *Human performance improvement* and *andragogy.*

3. HPI means making workers measurably more effective in their work. Effectiveness is usually measured in specific ways, such as the number of widgets produced per hour, the number of calls handled per hour, the number of products sold, or the number of errors. Three principles guide human performance improvement:

   • All training programs must produce measurable improvements in human behavior. Furthermore, these measurable improvements should offer tangible benefits to the organization sponsoring the training program.
   • Training programs address the gap between current and ideal performance.
   • Training might not fill the performance gap. It only fills gaps caused by a lack of skills and knowledge. Other causes include a lack of appropriate resources and a lack of motivation.

4. Principles of adult learning:

   • Adult learning is andragogy, not pedagogy.
   • Adult learners are pressed for time.
   • Adult learners are goal-oriented.
   • Adult learners bring previous knowledge and experience.
   • Adult learners have a finite capacity for information.
   • Adult learners have different motivation levels.
   • Adult learners have different learning styles, such as learn-then-do or do-then-learn.

5. ADDIE is an acronym that stands for analysis, design, development, implementation, and evaluation. Specifically, ADDIE involves:

   • Analysis, which refers to the activities performed for understanding the training problem and defining the objectives the training course should achieve. Analysis involves researching the problem, defining the objectives, and preparing the assessment.
   • Design, through which trainers determine how to present that content. Specifically, design involves choosing the form of the content, designing the presentation of the content, and choosing the elements of consistency in the course.
   • Development, through which trainers convert design plans into course materials. Specifically, development involves preparing course materials, and testing and reproducing them.

- Implementation, through which trainers bring the course to learners. Implementation involves scheduling courses, arranging for ongoing classroom support, and marketing and maintaining courses.
- Evaluation, though which trainers assess whether the courses have achieved their objectives. Evaluation occurs on these four levels: (1) satisfaction, (2) learning, (3) transfer to the job, and (4) business results.

This chapter introduced you to some of the basic principles of instructional design. Chapter 2 prepares you for the realities of an instructional design project. It identifies the people who participate in the project, and explains how to plan a project—the issues you need to consider and what you need to know to estimate the schedule and budget.

2

The Basics of Planning a Training Project

==

What's Inside This Chapter

This chapter introduces you to the basics of planning the schedule and budget for a training project—that is, an effort to design and develop a training course. Specifically this chapter addresses the following:

▶ Who needs to be a part of your training project team and what each will contribute to the project
▶ Issues to address when planning a schedule for your training project
▶ How to realistically estimate the cost of your project.

In addition, worksheets at the end of this chapter can help you plan a project.

Because training projects happen within a business context, before you begin designing and developing a training course, you need to address three key business questions that regularly arise during the project:

▶ Who will be involved in the design and development of your training program?

    ▶ When will you finish the program?

    ▶ How much will the program cost?

The following sections explain why these questions are so important to organizations and suggest how you can respond to them.

Who Works on a Training Project?

Although as course designer and developer you have primary responsibility for developing training programs, many people take an interest in your work. Each has a different concern about the project. For example, you may have a senior vice president anxiously anticipating a training course on a new management policy or a graphic designer waiting for a draft to begin making slides for the project. Perhaps a project manager is waiting for the number of hours spent on the project to ensure you have not gone over budget.

In other words, although your work might seem solitary at any given moment, designing and developing effective training programs involves collaboration among many professionals. One of your challenges is figuring out whom to consult when, and how to blend the people and their roles into an effective work team.

Project participants fall into two categories: members of the sponsoring organization and members of the training organization. The following sections describe each category of roles, describe the specific roles that people play, and offer suggestions for building a successful work team.

Roles Within the Sponsoring Organization

Whether working in an internal training department or for an external corporation, most trainers work in a client-like relationship. That is, someone outside of the training organization usually requests that you design and develop a course. The training program is intended to meet the needs of that client. For example, a manager of manufacturing might ask the training department to prepare a course on safety procedures; the vice president of marketing and sales might ask the training department to prepare an orientation for new sales representatives; or an outside company might contract yours to prepare a product training video.

In this book, the client is called the *sponsor*. The sponsor's representatives might each serve in just one role or one person might serve in several. The level of involvement also varies, depending on the combinations of roles that sponsor's representatives play, other responsibilities they have, and their interest in the project. Some play a central role in a project; others only play a role on paper. These roles are described in the sections that follow.

Paying Client. This person (also called the executive sponsor or benefactor) is the executive who has responsibility for the project. Although you won't have much contact with this person, recognize that because he or she is the one who can either authorize or stop payment for the project, the paying client is the one who must ultimately be satisfied with the results.

Subject Matter Experts (SMEs). This category includes one or more people who developed the technical content to be addressed by the training program. Your project may have one or more SMEs, depending on the type of training project and the size of your organization. See table 2-1 to see the types of SMEs involved in different types of training projects.

Table 2-1. Training and subject matter experts.

Type of Training	Typical SMEs
Product Training	Engineers, programmers, and scientists who designed and developed the product. In many organizations, marketing professionals who have played a role in developing and marketing the product also serve as SMEs.
Marketing Training	Marketing managers and staff (that is, people who develop sales strategies, create promotional programs, and oversee the salespeople in the field). In some cases, you may also consult with sales representatives in the field.
Management Development	Members of the HR staff and other managers who have responsibility for overseeing company policies, employee supervision, and succession planning.
Medical Training	Medical staff, engineers, and others involved in the service or product. For regulated products and services, members of the government regulation agency, such as the U.S. Food and Drug Administration, may also serve as an external SME.
New Employee Orientation	Members of the HR staff and managers from areas addressed in the training.
Manufacturing Training	Engineers who designed the manufacturing process and managers of the manufacturing lines affected.

Subject matter experts usually focus on the completeness and accuracy of the content in the training program. They are concerned that you precisely report information; a misused word often raises their concern. Often, SMEs request that you include more information than learners need, even though superfluous information could distract learners from successfully completing the objectives of the course. In such instances, you need to exercise your judgment about which information benefits learners and which does not, and then you have to diplomatically advocate for the needs of the learners.

Legal Staff. A representative of the corporate legal department can serve in this capacity. The legal reviewer verifies the accuracy of actual or implied promises and warranties in the program, checks for the proper use of intellectual property (such as trade or company secrets), and ensures that tests are fair for all learners.

Learners. The learners are the people who will take the training program. You precisely identify the learners when analyzing the needs for the program (see chapter 3 for more details). Learners primarily focus on the usefulness of the content to their own work and the ease of taking the course. Some of the issues that learners consider as they go through a training program are:

▶ Was the content easy to understand? Could learners understand the information on the first explanation or did they have to hear it several times before understanding?
▶ Was the information complete? Did learners find the answer to the entire question or did they have to ask follow-up questions to receive a satisfactory answer? Was something left out?
▶ Was the information relevant? Could learners figure out how to apply the content to their jobs?
▶ Could learners perform the skills taught when they returned to the job?
▶ How satisfied were learners with the training experience? If dissatisfied, what specifically caused issues for them?

Roles Within the Training Organization

The process of designing and developing training programs requires the skills of a variety of specialists. These specialists include the following.

Basic Rule 4

You work for the sponsor. Without the sponsor, you would have no work, so one of your chief jobs is pleasing the sponsor while remaining an advocate for the learner. That position presents some challenges because the needs of learners and the sponsor sometimes seem at odds. Nevertheless, the executive sponsor is only able to achieve his or her business needs if learners master the content. Ultimately, the two groups need one another.

▶ *Manager:* The person within the organization for whom you work that has overall responsibility for a project. Managers assign projects, establish budgets and schedules, secure resources for a project (such as computers and prototypes of products), and resolve problems with projects in progress. Sometimes they perform these tasks for you, other times managers work with you to perform these tasks. In some organizations, the manager might also serve as your supervisor. However, in other organizations, the manager only manages projects (called a *project manager*).

▶ *Curriculum planner:* The person who plans all of the training in a particular subject area, determining which courses to include, the content that each course covers, related materials, resources needed to develop this content, and overseeing the success of courses. A series of related training programs and materials in a given content area is called a *curriculum.* Sometimes, the curriculum planner and project manager are the same person.

▶ *Course designer and developer:* The person who performs the needs analysis; chooses and sequences content; drafts the slides, instructor's notes, and workbooks; and oversees production of the course materials. In many instances, course designers and developers have responsibility for the financial success of courses. Frequently, course designers and developers also teach the programs that they develop.

▶ *Graphic designer:* The person who designs the physical appearance of the training materials and prepares art work.

▶ *Illustrator:* The person who prepares specialized drawings, such as medical illustrations and drawings of new products.

▶ *Production personnel:* The people who prepare training materials for duplication. The skills needed for production vary, depending on the communications medium of the final product and may include desktop publishing, video, and audio skills. See table 2-2 for specific notes on these skills.

▶ *Training administrator:* The person who oversees the running of training programs, including promotional activities, scheduling of classrooms and instructors, enrollment, attention to learners during a course, recording courses completed by learners, and compiling evaluations.

Noted

People often confuse graphic designers and illustrators. Illustrators draw things, and graphic designers plan the overall appearance of text and illustrations.

In an ideal project, different people assume each of these different roles, letting each member focus on his or her area of expertise. On the typical project, however, one person assumes several roles. For example, the course designer and developer might also handle all of the production responsibilities for a training program. Note, too, that members of the team usually work on several projects simultaneously. As a result, people might not be available to work on your project when

Table 2-2. Specialized skills of production personnel.

Medium	Production Skills Needed
Printed Materials	Desktop publishing skills using software and hardware designated by the organization.
Online Materials	Authoring and programming skills. Authoring is the skill of using specialized software called authoring systems to prepare information for presentation online. Programmers assist with those situations when authoring systems cannot present information as the course designer and developer planned.
Video Presentations	Television production skills, which include camera and sound technicians, video editing (the process of taking various scenes, usually shot out of order, and assembling them onto a single videotape), acting, narration, and directing.
Audio Presentations	Sound production skills, which include narration and sound editing (compiling recordings made at separate times into a cohesive whole).

you need them. The sooner you can anticipate when you need the services of differ-ent team members, the better they can arrange their schedule to work when needed.

Effectively Working Together as a Team

Designing training is a team effort. Here are five suggestions that will help you and your team perform much more efficiently (Carliner, 1995):

1. Know yourself.
2. Before you start working together, spend some time getting to know one another.
3. Build respect for, and trust in, one another.
4. Initiate communication.
5. Be prepared for feedback.

Team work is more than sharing labor; it's sharing work. By following certain strategies at the beginning of a project, you increase the likelihood that the team will work together cohesively throughout the project.

Decisions. One of the most common problems in groups is members feeling that they have been left out of the decision-making process. So, before any major deci-sions are made, determine how you will make them. For example, do you plan to make decisions by consensus? By a vote? By deferring to a designated person? Each strategy has an appropriate place, as long as everyone is comfortable with it.

By openly discussing the decision-making process in your first meeting, you can avoid problems later. For example, if you have decided that all major decisions are to be made by consensus, then team members know that they should not be mak-ing unilateral decisions that affect the entire project, such as the format of all screens in a computer-based training program (Carliner, 1995).

Conflict. What happens if the group can't reach consensus on a decision? Do you not make a decision, defer to someone's judgment, or take a vote? And, what happens if two people can't work together? Does someone intervene? Do you let them work out the conflict by themselves?

Often, groups tend to avoid conflict and the unresolved issues rip apart their fabric. The people at the center of the fray often try to recruit other team members to their sides. Instead of a cohesive unit, the team becomes warring factions.

Deciding how to handle conflict before you actually experience it gives you a strategy for dealing with problems that arise (Carliner, 1995).

Commitment. Discuss the degree of commitment that you expect from each group member. Like most aspects of team work, each team member has a different concept of commitment. Some believe that commitment means giving 24 hours a day to the project. Others believe that commitment means full attention during work hours only. Still others believe that commitment involves weekend and late night work at times, but not for an indefinite stretch (Carliner, 1995).

Standards of Behavior. Until team members are fully comfortable with one another, encourage everyone to be on his or her best behavior. Some people, for example, are comfortable with off-color language and jokes. Others take great personal offense at them. Using conservative language and carefully avoiding discussions and expressions that might cause offense early in a project increases the likelihood of your acceptance by other teammates.

Nevertheless, the need for good behavior doesn't end once the group works together cohesively. Be careful to avoid taking other group members for granted following the period of good behavior. For example, don't assume that team members know that you appreciate their contributions because you have said so in the past.

Emphasize the importance of meeting all deadlines. Because people do not know whether they can trust one another early in a group relationship, a late project—late for whatever valid or invalid excuse—usually signifies a lack of commitment. It also breaches trust, because group members rely on each other to make commitments. If a group member fails to make a first commitment, other group members assume that the person is not trustworthy. Only later in the process are other group members willing to give some slack. For example, until people know what others are like, they cannot say, "It's not like him to miss a deadline" (Carliner, 1995).

Assumptions About Your Project

Before you plan the schedule and budget, you need to identify and state the assumptions upon which you are basing them. Doing so can help you manage the expectations of your sponsor. By managing those expectations, you are more likely to ensure the satisfaction of your sponsor.

There are a few common issues that affect the estimates of training projects. The first is the stability of subject matter. The less stable the subject matter, the more

Basic Rule 5

State your assumptions about a project up front. The budget and schedule for a successful project emerge from those assumptions. So before you make a commitment to complete a training course within a certain schedule and budget, identify and share with your sponsor the assumptions on which you make those promises. If these assumptions change later or prove incorrect, you can work with your sponsor to renegotiate the schedule and budget.

likely that you will need to completely revise sections that you have already written. By accounting for this instability in your planning, you help make your sponsor aware of the potential impact of changes. Focus on these issues:

▶ Identify, as specifically as possible, the aspects of the subject matter that are not stable.

▶ State what is not stable about the subject matter.

▶ Identify the sections affected by the unstable subject matter.

▶ Determine how to respond to the instability.

For example, you might double or triple your estimates of the schedule to provide you with suitable time to respond to unanticipated changes. Or, you might put conditions on the sponsor, stating that you must have certain issues resolved by certain dates or you reserve the right to miss your proposed schedule.

The second common issue that will most likely affect the estimate is the material that you do not intend to cover. Specifically state

Noted

By explicitly stating what you do not intend to cover, the sponsor is aware of another the limitations of the course. If the sponsor is not comfortable with the content being excluded, you can revise your design plans (and, as a result, budgets and schedules) now. Or, if your sponsor later asks you to add some of the material that you explicitly excluded, you have a basis for renegotiating the budget and schedule.

what it is. This should have been obvious from the design plans for the course, but the sponsor might only have noticed what you included, not what you excluded.

When Will You Finish the Program?

The schedule for a training program ultimately answers the question, "When will the program be ready?" Designing a training program is a complex project, requiring different pieces—such as the slides, instructor's guide, and student materials—that you might develop separately to come together at one time. In addition, you must have some assurance that the materials really work. For these reasons, development of a training program involves a series of intermediate steps (called *milestones* or *checkpoints*) so that the project is handled in manageable steps.

Basic Rule 6

Setting the proposed schedule involves performing the following activities in this order:

1. Estimating the size of the project.
2. Estimating the total length of the project (in number of workdays).
3. Establishing intermediate deadlines.

Estimating the Size of the Project

When assigning projects to design and develop training programs to be taught in the classroom, many sponsors and project managers also tell you the intended length of the course, such as a half-day, one day, two days, or a week. When planning such a project, assume that the length of the course is accurate. (Be sure to make note of this assumption.) If you find that you have too much or too little material for the intended length, then you might suggest a change in length after you plan the project.

When designing workbooks, you are often expected to estimate the length of a project (in pages). Experienced course designers and developers can suggest a length, based on the length of similar projects they have designed and developed in the past. If, however, you do not have experience, the best time to estimate the length of a project is after you have prepared the design for the training program. At that point, you have an idea of exactly which content will be included, how you will present it, and how many pages you need to present the material.

Unfortunately, most sponsors would like an estimate of the schedule for a project before you prepare the designs. In those instances, you must take your best guess. Then, you add a fudge factor to account for the uncertain nature of your guess. Use the fudge factor to increase the size of your project. The fudge factor varies, depending on a variety of conditions (table 2-3).

Table 2-3. Fudge factors for training projects.

If You Are Dealing With:	Add the Following Amount of Time to Your Schedule as a Fudge Factor:
Extremely stable subject matter	10 to 20 percent
Somewhat stable subject matter	20 to 30 percent
Unstable subject matter or an unreliable sponsor	As much as 50 to 100 percent

For example: Suppose that you estimate a workbook will consist of 100 pages. You assess that the subject matter is somewhat stable. According to table 2-3, you should add a 30 percent fudge factor:

To compute the 30 percent fudge factor:

$$100 \text{ pages} \times 0.30 \text{ (fudge factor)} = 30 \text{ pages}$$

Add the fudge factor to the page estimate:

$$100 \text{ pages} + 30 \text{ pages} = 130 \text{ total pages}$$

Therefore, the estimated number of pages (including fudge factor) is 130.

Estimating the Total Length of the Project in Workdays

Determine the total number of workdays needed for the project. Note that a workday is not the same as a regular day. Although a week contains seven days, it only contains five workdays. In this step, you calculate the total number of workdays needed to complete the project.

Think About This

How you compute the number of workdays necessary for your project depends on whether you set the deadline or if your sponsor sets an inflexible deadline.

When You ***Set the Deadline.*** This situation is ideal. You can establish the final deadline for the project based on the amount of time needed to complete the project. To compute the total number of workdays needed using this method, you use an estimate based on the medium of instruction.

The following rates provided are just suggestions because actual rates vary among organizations. Your time will almost certainly vary, but until you have experience, these estimates will provide you some realistic means of measurement:

- ▶ classroom courses: 25 to 40 hours of work for every finished hour of instruction. (Yes, 25 to 40 hours for just one finished hour of instruction!)
- ▶ workbook-based courses: four to six hours of work for every finished page in a workbook.

Figure 2-1 shows an example calculation for calculating the time necessary to complete a training project.

When Your Sponsor Has an Inflexible Final Deadline. When sponsors approach you to develop a training program, they often have an inflexible final deadline when they need for you to have the finished program available. This is called a *drop-dead date.* In such instances, the firm deadline must be the final deadline.

Noted

The fundamental concept underlying each of the estimating formulas is the concept of "finished" work. A finished page represents all the work involved in preparing the page: review time, management time, editing time, and preparation of graphics—not just the time of the course designer and of the developer. In addition, these time estimates include the time needed to prepare student materials used in the course.

Figure 2-1. Calculating the duration of a training project.

Total Days Needed to Complete a Classroom Course

Rate (25 to 40 hours of work for every completed hour of instruction) × number of hours

Assume that the course lasts 1.5 days. Also assume that one day of instruction results in 6.5 hours of actual contact time in the classroom (the rest of the eight hours is spent on breaks). Therefore, the actual length of the course in hours is:

$1.5 \times 6.5 = 9.75$ hours of instruction

Because the course designer and developer has some familiarity with the content, assume that work progresses at a rate of 35 hours of work for a finished hour of instruction (slightly lower than the 40 hours recommended).

9.75 hours of instruction × 35 hours of work per finished hour of instruction = 341.25 hours of completed work (by everyone).

How many workweeks are involved? To get the basic number of workweeks, divide the total number of hours—in this case 341.25—into workweeks: just under 8.6 weeks.

But you have not yet considered time away for holidays, sick leave, and other purposes. Add 20 percent to your estimate to arrive at the total number of workweeks needed to complete the project:

$(8.6 \times 0.2) + 8.62 = 10.32$ weeks

The total number of weeks estimated for this project is 10.32 weeks.

All the same, compute the total time needed to complete the project as you would using the other method. Although you might not have all of this time available to design and develop your training course, you might be able to use this information to request assistance in completing the project.

For example, suppose that the sponsor needs the course just described in eight weeks, even though you have estimated that the project needs about 10. By making the sponsor aware that you have removed 2.3 weeks from the schedule (about 25 percent of the total time of the project), you might need 25 percent or more of another resource to compensate for the lost time. It is important to note, however, that adding another person for the duration of the project is not equivalent to having someone on board for the entire project. A person might be available to fill in for the 25 percent of the time, but he or she also needs to be trained and kept informed about the project, which adds to the time needed.

Establishing Intermediate Deadlines

The calculation you just made indicated the *total* time needed to develop the training course. This time includes not only the time needed for drafting the program, but also for conducting the needs analysis, copying and distributing review drafts, conducting a trial run of the course, and producing the course materials. The time includes not just your time, but also the time invested by others, such as SMEs who review it, the graphic designer who produces the slides, and the production assistants who help produce and duplicate the materials.

Your next challenge is to identify the intermediate deadlines so that each person has sufficient time to do his or her job. These intermediate deadlines are called *milestones.* The phases in the process described in chapter 1 represent most of the milestones; but additional milestones are included because they alert various people who play a role in the process of developing a training course that their assistance is needed.

The amount of time assigned to each step is a percentage of time of the total project (Hackos, 1994). To assign intermediate deadlines, then, you would divide the time between now and the final deadline into four main chunks. Table 2-4 provides some suggestions for estimating the time needed for intermediate deadlines.

Assuming that you have 11 weeks to design and develop the course described earlier, your schedule would look like that shown in table 2-5.

Next, you assign specific dates to each activity. Although this activity is straightforward, for the most part, make sure that if you are conducting reviews online, you leave some time at either end of the review process for distribution (a half-day for a short course like this one). Networks often deliver files the moment you transmit them, but networks sometimes clog up and don't deliver your files to the intended receiver for several hours.

If you are conducting reviews with printed materials, make sure you leave sufficient time to copy the draft (at least two days, even with quick-copy services) and send it to reviewers (at least another two days, even with expedited mailing) and for reviewers to return the draft to you (at least another two days). (A tight schedule like this example leaves little time for copying and mailing.)

The bulk of the time needed for production is needed for producing the course materials, but some time is also included for printing.

Finally, notice that there's a fair amount of flexibility in assigning dates; the estimating formulas are just that—for estimating.

Table 2-4. Figuring intermediate deadlines.

Milestone	Percentage of Total Project
Needs analysis: Although you do not separately schedule them (you just schedule a single needs analysis), the schedule needs to leave time for performing each of these activities: • Research • Interviews • Report of the needs analysis • Approval for the report • Write objectives • Prepare evaluation plan • Receive informal approval for the objectives and evaluation plan	10 percent to 15 percent
Design: Although you will only schedule time for a draft of the design, a review, and a revision, make sure that the schedule leaves time to perform the following activities • Choosing form and medium • Structuring content • Preparing design plans • Reviewing and revising the design plans with the sponsor and potential learners • Preparing production guidelines (editorial, technical, production, and usability guidelines) • Final approval for the project plan	15 percent to 20 percent
First draft	25 percent
First review by SMEs and peers in your organization: Be realistic with review time; people cannot review 600 slides in a day or two. Also, make sure that you leave time for copying (if distributing printed review copies) and mailing (to and from you) as well as time for meetings to clarify review comments.	Part of the total time of developing the first draft, but you need to inform reviewers when copies are going to be sent.

(continued on page 32)

Table 2-4. Figuring intermediate deadlines (continued).

Milestone	Percentage of Total Project
Second draft	15 percent
Second review	Part of the total time of developing the second draft
Third draft (optional)	10 percent
Third review (optional)	Part of the total time of developing the third draft
Final draft	5 percent
Production: Although not separately reported in a schedule, leave sufficient time for: • Copyediting • Preparation of materials for printing • Printing	10 percent
Shipping and distribution of materials	1 to 4 additional weeks, depending on publishing method

Table 2-5. Time needed for design and development.

Milestone	Percentage of Total Project	Length of Time Needed
Needs Analysis	10 percent to15 percent	1 week
Design	15 percent to 20 percent	2 weeks
First Draft	25 percent	2.5 weeks
First Review	Part of the total time of developing the first draft	Set aside 3 days of the 2.5 weeks spent developing the first draft
Second Draft	15 percent	1.5 weeks
Second Review	—	Set aside 2 days of the 1.5 weeks
Third Draft (Optional)	10 percent	1 week
Third Review (Optional)	—	Set aside 1 day of the 1 week
Final Draft	5 percent	0.5 week
Production	10 percent	1.5 weeks
Shipping and Distribution	1-4 weeks	1 week

As you review the proposed schedule with your sponsor, ask him or her for a signed commitment to complete all reviews as scheduled. This commitment is necessary because your schedule depends on your sponsor completing reviews at the scheduled time. If the sponsor does not meet a scheduled review date, ask for a written commitment that you have the right to delay final completion of the project one workday for each workday the reviews are delayed.

Once you have a committed schedule, publish it and make sure everyone on the project team is aware of it. Regularly remind team members of upcoming deadlines so that you have the assistance you need, at the time you need it.

Basic Rule 7
Set the budget after setting the schedule.

How Much Is the Program Going to Cost?

A budget is an itemized estimate of the cost of producing the project. Because the most significant cost is labor, and you pay for labor by the amount of time that you use it, much of the budget is based on the length of the project, which you determine when you estimate the schedule. The cost of designing and developing a training program includes a fully "burdened" cost of the course designer and developer, project manager, and production staff.

Noted

A "burdened" cost includes both the cost of labor and additional "burden" costs; that is, the fully burdened cost includes the salary as well as benefits (if any), employment taxes (if any), and related overhead expenses (such as the cost of the office, cost of support services).

In addition are costs for equipment, software, training, duplication, and the cost of specialized services. Different organizations use different methods for computing these costs. For example, some organizations have an hourly rate that they charge for a course designer and developer that also includes the costs of the project manager. Others separately charge for these services.

Table 2-6 shows an example estimate for the training program whose schedule was estimated in the previous section. Note that this estimated budget in the example only covers the cost of designing and developing the program, and duplicating the course materials. It does not include the cost of teaching the training program. Furthermore, this estimated budget does not include the cost of reviewers' time except for specialists whom you might contract with.

When you have developed your budget, review it with the sponsor. Once you have your sponsor's approval, you can use the budget as a basis for spending on this project.

Table 2-6. Example of a budget calculation.

Budget Item	Time and Rate	Total
Fully "burdened" cost of course designer and developer	10.3 weeks @$85/hour	$35,020
Fully burdened cost of the project manager, about 15 percent of the total time of the project	1.5 weeks @ $100/hour	$6,000
Fully burdened cost of the production staff, about 15 percent of the total time of the project	1.5 weeks @ $100/hour	$6,000
Costs of specialized services, such as the cost of conducting a usability test	Guesstimate	$10,000
Equipment costs, such as the purchase or lease of a special computer for the project	None on this project	0
Software costs, such as the purchase or lease of an authoring system or graphics software	None on this project	0
Training costs associated with the project	One 1-week class out of town	$3,800 ($2,000 for tuition, $1,800 in travel expenses)
Copying and distribution costs for review drafts	Will be handled electronically	0
Production costs, such as the cost of preparing special printing plates	Special setup for cover of the student materials	$1,000
Duplicating costs for the final product, which your printer can provide	100 pages, $.07/page, $2/copy for covers and binding, 450 copies	$4,050
Total		**$65,870**

Think About This

When preparing a budget, also prepare for problems to arise either during the budgeting process or after the sponsor approves the budget. These potential problems include:

- *unanticipated costs:* This category includes, for example, permission fees for using illustrations and graphics in a course unless the materials were produced by a staff illustrator. Most course designers and developers usually forget to budget for these.
- *underestimated costs:* Here's an example: When estimating the budget, you assumed that you needed 450 copies of the student materials but you actually needed 925. The cost of the additional copies is unanticipated.
- *scope creep:* Scope creep refers to a situation in which a project increases in scope after you estimate the budget and schedule. Because the additional scope creeps up (usually, a bit at a time), it is called scope creep. Scope creep results either from failing to understand the actual scope of work required by the project or by making wrong assumptions.

Some proven ways to address these problems are

- *fudge factors:* A fudge factor is an additional percentage built into a project to give you additional funding should unanticipated problems arise. This is also called a *contingency*. Different organizations have different levels of contingency.
- *tracking:* By carefully tracking how closely schedules and budgets match their estimates, you can notify sponsors early if you anticipate problems and negotiate for additional resources or, in the case of scope creep, return the project to its original scope.

Getting It Done

This section contains three worksheets (exercises 2-1, 2-2, and 2-3) that you can use to begin planning a training project.

Exercise 2-1. Staffing a training project.

Roles Within the Sponsoring Organization

Identify some candidates within and outside your organization who could serve on your training project team.

- Paying client (also called the executive sponsor or benefactor): _____
  _____
- SMEs: _____
- Legal: _____
- Learners: _____

Roles within the Training Organization

- Manager: _____
- Course designer and developer: _____
- Graphic designer: _____
- Illustrator: _____
- Production personnel: _____
- Training administrator: _____
- Curriculum planner: _____

Considerations

- Do people play one or more roles?
- Availability of staff when needed?
- Other projects to which staff are assigned?
- How well do the skills and abilities of people proposed for roles match the skills and abilities really needed in those roles?

Exercise 2-2. Scheduling a training project.

Based on your knowledge of the project deadline (whether set by you or by the sponsor) and on the guidelines listed below, set some milestone dates.

Milestone	Percentage of Total Project	Date
Needs analysis: Usually not indicated as separate milestones but need to be accounted for in your planning: • Research • Interviews • Report of the needs analysis • Approval for the report • Write objectives • Prepare evaluation plan • Receive informal approval for the objectives and evaluation plan	10 percent to 15 percent	
Design: Usually not indicated as separate milestones but need to be accounted for in your planning: • Choosing form and medium • Structuring content • Preparing design plans • Reviewing and revising the design plans with the sponsor and potential learners • Preparing production guidelines (editorial, technical, production, and usability guidelines) • Final approval for the project plan	15 percent to 20 percent	
First draft	25 percent	

Activity	Time
First review by SMEs and peers in your organization	Part of the total time of developing the first draft
Second draft	15 percent
Second review	Part of the total time of developing the second draft)
Third draft (optional)	10 percent
Third review (optional)	Part of the total time of developing the third draft
Final draft	5 percent
Production. Although not separately reported in a schedule, leave sufficient time for: • Copyediting • Preparation of materials for printing • Printing	10 percent
Shipping and distribution of materials	1–4 additional weeks, depending on publishing method

Exercise 2-3. Budgeting for a training project.

As you complete this budgeting worksheet, remember that you must consider both potential problems (including unanticipated costs and underestimated costs) and scope creep. Scope creep can result from failure to understand the scope of work, wrong assumptions, and incomplete information. To compensate for these "gotchas," remember these solutions: fudge factors, tracking, and early notification of milestones and deadlines. See table 2-6 for additional guidance, if needed.

Budget Item	Time and Rate (number of hours and rate per hour)	Total Cost
Fully burdened cost of course designer and developer		
Fully burdened cost of the project manager, about 15 percent of the total time of the project		
Fully burdened cost of the production staff, about 15 percent of the total time of the project		
Costs of specialized services, such as the cost of conducting a usability test		
Equipment costs, such as the purchase or lease of a special computer for the project		
Software costs, such as the purchase or lease of an authoring system or graphics software		
Training costs associated with the project		
Copying and distribution costs for review drafts		
Production costs, such as the cost of preparing special printing plates		
Duplicating costs for the final product, which your printer can provide		
Total		

This chapter explored how to plan the budget and schedule for a training project. The next chapter shows you how to begin work on such a project. It describes the six basic issues you need to explore when beginning a project, and how to collect this information.

3

The Basic Information Needed to Start a Project

■ ■

What's Inside This Chapter

This chapter introduces you to the basic information that you need to start work on a training project. It includes:

▶ The six basic issues about which you need information as you embark on a training project
▶ Some effective ways to track down this information.

In addition, a worksheet at the end of this chapter helps structure the information-gathering process for you.

Six Basic Needs Analysis Steps

When new course designers and developers first start a project, many immediately rush to work on slides, quizzes, student workbooks, and similar materials. After all, sponsors often provide course designers and developers with the particulars: the audience, the material that the course needs to cover, and the date when you need to complete the project. Therefore, work on the training course can commence. Right?

Wrong.

Although sponsors provide you with information about the project, it might not be complete enough for your purposes. It might be incorrect. It might reflect an incomplete understanding of the learners or the content.

Consider this: a course designer and developer was assigned to prepare product training for new software. When assigned to this project, the SMEs said that two-thirds of the market for this product was hospital staffs and the other third of the market was universities. After checking with the marketing department, this course designer and developer learned that few people in universities actually used the software. Universities made up about 60 percent of the market and manufacturers accounted for most of the remaining 40 percent of the market. Had she not verified the information, her course would have been geared toward an incorrect audience.

Basic Rule 8

Always begin a training project by conducting a needs analysis. Even if the sponsor believes that the information already provided is complete, verify it because the sponsor collected it for purposes other than training. Also, you might need to collect additional information that the sponsor did not need.

To avoid a situation similar to the one with the course just described (the one intended for hospitals and universities, but used by universities and manufacturing organizations), start a training project by first verifying the information that you received, then filling in missing, but useful, information. Specifically, you need to learn about the following categories of issues:

- ▸ the request itself
- ▸ the business need underlying the project
- ▸ the desired performance
- ▸ the tasks
- ▸ the learners and the influences on them
- ▸ the constraints on the project.

The process of gathering this information is called a *needs analysis*. This chapter targets the information you need to collect in a needs analysis.

Also, before starting work on a project, you need to identify the objectives that the project must achieve and develop tests to assess whether learners have met those objectives (yes, you write the test before designing and developing the course). The next chapter explores objectives and tests.

Issue 1. Restate and Clarify the Request

The first step in analyzing the needs underlying a request to develop a course is restating the request.

Basic Rule 9

When restating the training request, use the exact words that the sponsor has used.

When you restate the training request using the exact words, consider this. If a sponsor has asked you to develop a "two-part sales training course, one of which focuses on the product and another that focuses on techniques for relationship marketing," you would begin this part by stating that you have been asked to develop a "two-part sales training course, one of which focuses on the product and another that focuses on techniques for relationship marketing." You might expand on the request after quoting the sponsor's predefined specifications verbatim.

Starting the project by using the exact same words that the sponsor used is a way of letting him or her know that you listened carefully to the request and understood exactly the sponsor's meaning. Few things build trust the way that type of listening does. Repeating the request using the sponsor's words does not mean that the final project must take the form of the request. For example, if a sponsor requests that you design and develop a one-week classroom course, but you believe that the sponsor's needs would be best served by creating a preclass workbook and a two-day classroom course, the sponsor is more likely to comply with your suggestions if he or she believes that you understand the initial request.

In addition, as you restate the request, clarify it to make sure that you fully understand it. Clear up all questions about the specific request or the intended learners at this point. Although inquiry about other areas also explores these issues, by clarifying now, you make sure that you're asking questions about the right issues.

When restating the request, also include key parts of the request that affect course design. Here are some examples (note that these examples will be expanded upon throughout this and the next several chapters):

- The vice president of marketing and sales has requested a one-week classroom-based sales school and a series of workbooks to address prerequisite materials and postclass content. The sales school will be required of new sales representatives and must cover relationship marketing, marketing policies, and ordering procedures, and it must provide an overview of the current product line.
- The manager of internal software applications has requested a half-day training course for end users of the new accounts receivable application. The course must launch May 2, about three weeks before the new application goes live.
- The chief security officer has requested a two-hour classroom-based training course for managers about the new security policy. The course must launch in eight weeks, when new security procedures begin.

Issue 2. Identify the Business Need Underlying the Request

Dana and James Robinson (1989) advise training and HPI professionals that managers and executives are most likely to value their efforts and that these efforts are most likely to effect change, if they are directly tied to a business need.

Basic Rule 10
Begin each course by identifying the business goal before you have even determined which content to include.

In practical terms, this means that a training program is most likely to have impact if it addresses a revenue or cost problem that the business currently faces and if the use of the information taught in the course is tied to the measurements of effectiveness for the staff of the organization.

The best time to create this linkage is at the very beginning of an effort to develop a training program, before you even consider its content. At this point, the effort should be tied to one—and only one—of the three categories of business goals, as presented in table 3-1.

Table 3-1. The three types of business goals.

Business Goal	Training Projects Relevant to the Business Goal
Generating Revenue	Some proposed training programs are associated with efforts to generate revenue for the organization. For example, sales representatives usually participate in product training courses so they can sell those products.
Containing Expenses	Some proposed training programs are intended to increase staff productivity, reduce the number of errors, or increase self-sufficiency (so users do not need costly, in-person help). For example, user training for software is intended to reduce user reliance on more costly support services, such as a help line. A refresher course on manufacturing is often intended to reduce errors in the manufacturing process.
Complying With Regulations	Some proposed training programs are required by government, industry, or corporate guidelines. For example, one course required by many governments is the Right to Know course, which informs workers of dangerous chemicals in their workplaces, and how to work with those chemicals. Organizations that fail to provide compliance training risk stiff fines or can even be shut down by regulatory authorities.

Be firm about choosing one—and only one—to address with a given training project. Many sponsors would like a single training program to address several business needs. Like most things that try to do too much, a double focus increases the risk of it failing to succeed with either need.

Also, state the business result as tangibly as possible when the goal is being identified. For example, if you have been asked to develop a course that supports a sales effort, the business goal might be meeting the sales projections. Similarly, if you have been asked to develop a course to comply with an occupational safety and health regula-

Noted

The business goal should not be confused with the business case. The business case is an economic justification for producing the course. The business goal is just one part of that case.

tion, your goal might be 100 percent compliance with the regulation. The more tangible the result, the more likely that sponsors will see the benefit of the completed course.

The type of business goal often suggests the relative budget available for the training program. Generally, a training program that is intended to generate revenue has a large budget, a program intended to contain revenue has a medium-sized budget, and a program intended to comply with regulations has a limited budget.

Here are three examples of business goals that were described previously in the chapter:

> ▶ *A business goal associated with generating revenue:* After completing the proposed sales school, 90 percent of new marketing representatives will meet their first-year revenue goals.

> ▶ *A business goal associated with containing expenses:* After completing the training course for the new accounts receivable application, 85 percent of workers in the accounts receivable organization will transfer to the new application by June 1, thus reducing application support costs by 10 percent.

> ▶ *A business goal associated with compliance:* After completing the training course on the new security policy, the organization will have 100 percent compliance with the new security procedures when they launch.

Issue 3. Identify the Desired Performance

The difference between current performance and the ideal performance is called the *performance gap.* Effective training bridges the performance gap. Ultimately, an effective training program must close the performance gap by affecting the way that learners perform their jobs. To make sure that your training program builds that desired performance, one of the first issues to consider when learning about the content is getting a description of the end result—what ideal performance looks like.

Determine what ideal performance looks like by asking the sponsor to describe the performance indicators he or she hopes that learners will demonstrate after successfully completing the training program. Here are the performance indicators for the examples identified earlier:

> ▶ *New sales school:* Using their knowledge of the entire product line, sales representatives will use relationship marketing techniques to sell all relevant products to their assigned customers and generate follow-up sales from at least 50 percent of those customers within one year. In addition, sales representatives

Basic Rule 11

Before you determine what to teach, you first need to determine what successful performance looks like.

will properly complete order forms to ensure that customers receive products within the timeframe promised by distributors.

▶ *New accounts receivable application:* Users will transfer their accounting information to the new system by June 1 and will use the system self-sufficiently by June 15 (that is, requiring no more than 0.5 calls for assistance per month).

▶ *New security policy:* Confidential material will not be leaked. More specifically, all written confidential material will be properly labeled (both online and in print). All confidential material will be locked in desks or credenzas, even in secured areas. No confidential material will be discussed in public areas. To gain access to all confidential material on internal computers, users will have to enter a password.

By beginning at the end—desired performance—you always keep that goal in sight as you design and develop the training program, and you can avoid covering irrelevant material.

If you are working on a training program to build on current performance (rather than introduce a new subject to learners), you can also identify the current performance. In other words, you would state what the potential learners are currently achieving and the process by which they reach those results.

For example, consider current performance for the three example courses described in this chapter:

▶ *New sales school:* Although the sales school is new, the company does hire new marketing representatives who go to work with limited coaching from their time-pressed managers. Right now, only 50 percent of marketing representatives achieve their sales targets, and only 10 percent receive repeat business.

 Think About This

At this time, you should also describe the environment in which people work. When attempting to understand why the learners are not performing in their ideal manner, the relevancy of this information becomes apparent. If you have several groups of learners performing the task in different ways, you might take several "before" pictures. These snapshots might also describe the work environment in which people perform the task and a bit about their motivations to do so.

Fifty percent of all marketing representatives leave the company within two years, causing the company to frequently replace its chief contact with customers. As a result, customers feel that the company does not value their business and repeat business is limited.

▶ *New accounts receivable application:* The new application uses a graphical user interface like that on a PC or Mac, replacing the character interface of the 30-year-old accounts receivable application. Also, under the present system, users must memorize numerous codes when entering transactions. To help remember the codes, most users have Post-It notes attached all around the sides of their screens. Still, about 12 percent of all transactions are entered with errors because the accounts receivable person used the wrong code.

▶ *New security policy:* Of the last three products, the plans for two were leaked in part to the trade press. Although the press cited anonymous sources, a private investigation determined that the leaks resulted from confidential information being posted on the company's publicly available intranet. Reporters then went to a coffee shop near the development lab and eavesdropped on product developers talking about their work on new products. From those conversations, the reporters were able to glean enough information to publish stories in the trade press.

Issue 4. Identify the Tasks in Desired Performance

In this area of inquiry, you try to identify the specific process (or processes) that learners must follow to achieve ideal performance.

Subject matter experts, especially expert performers, can help you identify the tasks that learners must perform. The tasks fall into three categories:

▶ Psychomotor tasks are those performed by hand or some other physical activity.

▶ Cognitive tasks are performed mentally, such as choosing the right model of computer to meet a customer's needs or matching symptoms with a diagnosis.

▶ Attitudinal, or *affective,* tasks are associated with learners' attitudes. Usually, affective tasks are redefined as cognitive or psychomotor tasks.

Basic Rule 12

Identify each task that someone must go through to achieve desired performance, so that you can address those tasks in the training program.

A thorough analysis of the process is called a *task analysis* because it identifies the tasks of the ideal process. Specifically, a task analysis identifies both the tasks that must be mastered to achieve peak performance as well as the tasks that learners are assumed to have mastered, which are called *entry tasks*. A thorough task analysis is often extremely detailed, literally breaking one large task into scores of subtasks. Each task begins with an action verb. An action verb describes a task that can be observed by an outside party. For example, the term *describe* is an action verb.

Tasks are presented as a hierarchy. At the top of the hierarchy are the most important tasks, called *main tasks*. A course typically covers between five and nine main tasks. It may have fewer, but if a course has more main tasks, the amount of material overwhelms learners. If you find that you have more than nine main tasks, consider combining main tasks.

Think About This

Avoid abstract verbs when writing tasks. Abstract verbs are ones that cannot be observed by an outside party. These include two terms closely associated with the learning business: know and understand. Replace these verbs with action verbs. For example, what can a learner do when they understand something? Can they explain? Describe? Define?

To perform one main task, learners must often master several related tasks, called *supporting tasks*. You should have between three and nine supporting tasks for each main task. Some supporting tasks, in turn, have additional supporting tasks.

The end product of a task analysis is a tree of sorts, which breaks the main task into many supporting tasks and breaks those supporting tasks into sub-supporting tasks, until the tasks cannot be subdivided any more.

Figure 3-1 shows a sample hierarchy for one main task. In this hierarchy, learners must master three supporting tasks to master the main task. Learners must have already mastered one entry task before starting this training program.

Performing a task analysis presents many challenges. One is the challenge of extracting information from experts. Some tasks are performed so routinely and so often that they become second nature. At that point, it becomes difficult for experts to describe in complete detail how they do them. Other experts are reluctant to share their expertise for fear that they'll lose their competitive advantage. In other instances, people disagree about the tasks, and you have to resolve the differences.

Figure 3-1. A hierarchy of tasks.

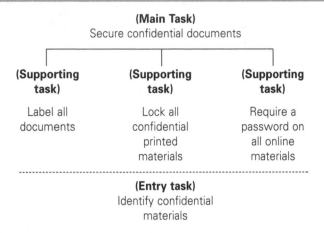

So many course designers and developers go through a task analysis several times with a SME to make sure that the list of tasks is complete. The experts might inadvertently leave an item off the list.

Issue 5. Describe the Learners and the Influences on Them

To design training so that it will be able to close a performance gap, it is necessary to collect a variety of information about the learners, including the following:

▸ *Demographic data:* This category of information includes items such as job title, length of experience, assumed knowledge, sex (if relevant), language skills (if relevant), cultural affiliations (if appropriate), and similar information.

▸ *Previous knowledge:* If learners have previous experience with the subject matter of the proposed course or with related material, describe it. As mentioned in chapter 1, effective adult learning experiences relate new content to known content; therefore, establishing links early helps you design a more effective learning experience. Additionally, you might find that, to master the new material, learners must unlearn old ways of performing tasks. You need to address this need and any related attitudes in your course.

▸ *Influences affecting the learners:* Some influences may come from the business, such as a recent reorganization that results in new work for a group. Some of these influences are cultural. For example, when two companies merge, they usually have different cultures that play a role in acceptance of learning programs. To be successful, you need to address these influences when you design the program.

Some training programs just have one primary group of learners, others serve several primary groups. If a program has several primary groups of learners, prepare separate descriptions for each group. That is, you would prepare a separate set of demographics for each group and separate sets of character descriptions. By separating these now, you can later see whether content for one group will be appropriate for another, or whether it might need to be adjusted. You might need to develop different sections of the training program for different groups of learners.

Table 3-2 shows some descriptions of learners for the three example courses mentioned earlier in this chapter.

Basic Rule 13

Collect enough information about learners to "know" them. The better you understand who your learners are, their previous experience, and their motivations, the better you can tailor the content to their needs.

Issue 6. Identify Constraints on the Project

Product Constraints. These constraints affect what you can present and how you can present it. Among them are the following:

- ▶ *Course structure:* Sometimes organizations establish a standard structure for certain types of courses. An example would be a standard outline for product training and management development courses. Some organizations require that you use certain slides, such as a standard title slide, an agenda slide, a slide that provides administrative details to learners, and a closing slide. Similarly, some organizations require that you include certain material in student workbooks, perhaps a standard title page, copyright notice, preface, or glossary. Find out which guidelines apply to make sure that your work conforms to them.
- ▶ *Editorial guidelines:* Also called style guidelines, these constraints affect the use of terminology, punctuation, and grammar. Most medium and large corporations have established style guides; the corporate communications

Table 3-2. Learner descriptions for the three example learning projects.

Type of Learning Project	Intended Learners
New sales school for new sales representatives	About 50 percent are new college hires (that is, hired directly out of college) with bachelor's degrees in business (the majority) and humanities and social sciences like psychology and history (the next largest group). These learners have no previous experience selling business-to-business products. Most have limited work experience from college internships and summer jobs.
	Thirty-five percent are transfers from within the company. All of these workers have at least a bachelor's degree (though the fields vary widely), and about 15 percent have master's degrees (though not in a relevant field). These people have extensive experience with company products from their work in customer support (the majority of workers), product development (the next largest group), and operations (the third largest group). However, most do not have any sales experience, and a majority has expressed concern about meeting their sales quota.
	Fifteen percent are professional hires (people with professional experience). Of these, 50 percent have previous sales experience; the other 50 percent have worked in either product development or marketing programs. Those with sales experience are not necessarily familiar with relationship marketing, though few would acknowledge that. They are also not familiar with the company product line or sales procedures.
New accounts receivable application for workers in the accounts receivable department	All have experience using the predecessor application, which used a character interface. The average tenure with the company is 15 years; of those, the average tenure in accounts receivable is eight years. All workers have at least a high-school education, most have at least two years of post-secondary education (many with an associate's degree). In addition, about two-thirds of workers say they have a home computer and use it on average twice a week. These employees also do not respond well to change. According to a personality test taken in conjunction with management training, 59 percent of the workers in accounts receivable have a compliant personality, one that works best with well-defined, stable rules.
New security policy training for everyone in the company	Employees encompass a wide range of education and skills, from high school dropouts to engineers with doctorates. They have all received training in identifying confidential data and passed a test certifying that they can recognize confidential data. Although all employees will receive this training, emphasis will be especially strong in product development areas, where employees typically do not respond well to structure and administration, as observed by managers who have had to implement similar policies in the past.

Basic Rule 14

In addition to identifying the performance gap, the tasks to be covered, and the learners, you must also identify the constraints affecting the project: product constraints, software (even for classroom courses and workbooks), business constraints, and corporate culture.

department usually chooses it. Most corporations also have a preferred dictionary and general style guide, from which they derived corporate guidelines. In most instances, training programs must conform to these style guidelines.

▶ *Design guidelines:* These constraints affect the design of slides and workbooks. Most corporations want a "family look" to everything they publish, so that material produced by many different groups within a company looks similar. Specifically, corporate design guidelines specify which typefaces you should use and when, margins, use of colors, use of images, the use of buttons and other standard elements on screens, use of the corporate logo, and similar issues. The corporate communications department usually maintains the corporate design guidelines.

▶ *Other standards and guidelines:* In some cases, your training program must resemble other courses or materials used by the organization. Or, one course is part of a larger series of courses and learning materials, like the Dummies books. If your course is supposed to have a family look, verify that fact early in the development process.

Software Constraints. Sometimes, you must also use certain software (called authoring tools) to create courses because your organization already owns licenses for certain software or because a sponsor requested its use. Specifically, you should identify which of the following software you are expected to use when developing the course:

▶ word processor (such as Microsoft Word or Corel WordPerfect)
▶ presentation program (such as Microsoft PowerPoint)
▶ desktop publishing program (such as QuarkXpress)
▶ graphics program (such as Adobe Illustrator or Photoshop)
▶ specialized software (such as software for capturing screenshots).

Business Constraints. The third set of constraints for your consideration includes

- the drop-dead deadline for completing the project
- the not-to-exceed budget
- staff who must participate in the design and development effort.

Constraints of Corporate Culture and the Learning Environment. The last set of constraints is one that you should not include in a report to sponsors. These are issues of corporate culture, the sponsor's history with previous projects that will affect your work, and aspects of the learning environment that will promote or hinder learning. These issues include

- *communication strategies within the organization:* Do people communicate directly and, if so, what are the channels, or do they communicate indirectly, and if so, how?
- *attitude toward the subject matter:* Does the organization embrace it or will people avoid it? Be honest, even though the sponsor will tell you that everyone welcomes the content.
- *project history:* Is the organization notorious for last-minute changes? If so, be prepared because it will happen again.
- *learning environment for self-study courses:* Where will learning occur? Is that environment conducive to learning? If not, what needs to change? Are there opportunities in the work environment to tie learning to work? Do managers and co-workers support learning? If so, how? If not, what do they do?

By identifying aspects of the corporate culture and the learning environment, you can assess the influence of your sponsor in the organization, the likelihood that technical information will change during the course of the project, and the behaviors you need to succeed in the organization. See figure 3-2 for an example of how a training program designer might identify constraints for a proposed course to train end users on a new software application for the accounts receivable department.

Four Methods of Uncovering Needs

One of the major challenges of a needs analysis is finding methods of uncovering the information—often with little time and support from others. You therefore need to determine where you can get the information quickly and easily because sponsors

Figure 3-2. Example analysis of project constraints.

Type of Constraint	Specific Considerations
Product Constraints	• Course structure: — Slides must follow the IT Course Template, which specifies standard typefaces and margins; bullet characters; and the following slides: title, agenda, objectives, classroom administration, closing slide, and list of related courses. — Student materials must follow the IT Student Materials Template, which stipulates standard typefaces and margins; bullet symbols; running headers and footers; and the following pages: title, table of contents, edition notice (copyrights), student evaluation form, and list of related courses. • Templates available from the lead application support representative. • Editorial guidelines: — Use the standard IT glossary. — Follow the *New York Times Manual of Style and Usage,* as amended for use within the organization. • Design guidelines: See material on templates.
Technical Constraints	• Slides: Microsoft PowerPoint • Student materials: Microsoft Word • Graphics: Adobe Photoshop • Software demos: Use the application. • Screen capture software: CaptureEze • Sample files for student exercises must be available. Weekly backups required of all files under development, in addition to those automatically made by the IT department.
Business Constraints	• Drop-dead date: May 2, three weeks before the new application goes live. • Not-to-exceed budget: Not stated, but no funds available for external services, such as an outside graphic designer or outside assistance with production. • Staff: Materials must be approved by the manager of internal software applications. Drafts must be reviewed by the following members of his or her staff: senior application designer, application programmers, and lead application support representative. They will make a recommendation on approval to the manager.
Corporate Culture and Project History	• This organization has a history of missing its projected deadlines. Of the last five introductions of new applications, the IT department only delivered one on time. The rest were late, varying from one week to nine weeks. • The IT department also has a history of making many last-minute changes. We need to anticipate at least 50 percent change on the second draft, based on previous history. • The IT department has a history of failing to communicate all the changes. Therefore, we should review the second draft with a walkthrough to make sure that all changes have been identified and will be included in the final draft.

often balk at the cost of conducting a full-scale needs analysis, even though you need more complete information to prepare a successful course.

Also keep in mind that when conducting a needs analysis, you ultimately want to *triangulate* information. That is, rather than relying on one source for all of your information (at the best, that source might not be complete and, at the worst, it might not be trustworthy), you want to collect information from a variety of sources, at least three. By looking at the content from these different vantages, you can construct a more realistic portrait of the reality. The following sections describe four ways you might be able to get the information you need quickly and easily.

1. Talk

Conduct formal interviews with as many people who have information to share as possible. Typically, these people include stakeholders, such as the sponsor, SMEs, and prospective learners. Other stakeholders probably have an interest in the proposed training program, too. The advantage is that many stakeholders will gladly meet with you and can give you an extensive amount of information in a limited period of time. The disadvantage is that the information received is biased, representing the viewpoint of the interviewee.

2. Focus Groups

Focus groups are a special type of interview, in which you interview eight to 12 demographically similar people at a single time. The focus group usually lasts two hours and can cover between three and five questions.

An outside facilitator usually leads the focus group and makes sure that each participant has an opportunity to speak. The advantage of a focus group is its efficiency; you can interview many people in less than the time it would take to interview two individuals. The disadvantage is that the participants are not able to exchange much information, and group pressure might prevent some from speaking honestly.

3. Experience

One of the ways to learn about a subject is to experience it. An efficient way of doing so is by following people through their daily routines from the start of the workday until the end.

This method is called "A Day in the Life" because it literally follows a day in the life of a worker. Course developers typically follow an expert, a novice, or both, in the performance of the tasks covered by the proposed course. The advantage of this approach is the hands-on nature of the experience and the depth to which a course developer can see the content in action. The disadvantages are the cost (especially if travel is required) and that the day only reflects one person's experience.

Note that if you only have part of a day, a little observation is better than none. In other words, if you don't have time for a day in the life, perhaps you have time for a few hours at least.

4. Read

In many cases, you do not need to conduct new research to uncover the information needed to start a training project—you merely need to find existing research. Therefore, one of the most valuable sources of content is the documents already available about the situation. Read anything that might provide useful insights into the content or the learners: reports, plans, policies, user's guides, memos and other

Think About This

"But, my SMEs are being tight-lipped." In some instances, SMEs do not willingly share content with you, even though they have a vested interest in the success of your training program. But you need the information, so be persistent and assertive. Here are some suggestions for overcoming specific objections:

1. "We have already done the research, you don't need to." Ask to see original source documents, so you can assess the original research for yourself. Chances are, you'll come to the same general conclusions, but you might see some additional relevant information in the documents that is not reflected in the summary provided to you.
2. "We cannot afford to send you to visit with learners." This objection often comes up with learners who are hourly employees or are external customers. In such instances, ask to talk to someone who has direct experience with the learners. After all, someone else's firsthand experience is the next best thing to meeting real learners.
3. "We have provided you with written documentation and we are so busy, that we do not have time to meet with you." Rather than asking for a first meeting, ask for a meeting to review the materials provided to you so that you can make sure that you understand the information provided.

correspondence, trade magazines, and even other training programs. The advantage of this method is that it unearths much good information. The disadvantage is that most people recognize that written records are permanent and prepare them so that they reflect most positively on the author.

One More Thing

Although the chapter describes six needs-analysis issues to explore, a list of areas only provides a starting point for your needs analysis. Because no two courses are alike, no single set of scripted questions can identify all of the needs underlying a project. Therefore, if you hear of something that you feel may be relevant, explore it.

Similarly, keep an open mind as you explore needs. If you enter a needs analysis with the solution already designed, then you will not ask the questions that might help you come up with the intervention best matched to meet the needs. In the same way, keep an open mind about the answers to the questions. Rather than entering this process for the purpose of confirming your answers, enter it to learn. You might find that your instincts are off. You have not yet developed the training program, so you can easily change strategies at this point.

Getting It Done

As you begin work on your training program, you need to investigate each of the issues of questioning, and choose an appropriate way to get the information you need. Use exercise 3-1 with a current project to track the results of the needs analysis.

Exercise 3-1. Needs analysis: six issues to consider.

Needs Analysis Issue	Actions Required	Information Source(s)
1. Restate the Request	Use the sponsor's words. _____ _____ For example: Create a training class for new users of Microsoft Project software.	• Sponsor _____ _____ _____
2. Identify the Business Need	This project will provide the following benefit to the sponsor (check one box only): ☐ Generate revenue ☐ Contain expenses ☐ Comply with regulations How will this training program provide this benefit to the sponsor? (Explain as tangibly as possible.) _____ _____	• Interviews (list individuals) _____ _____ _____ • Documents (list them) _____ _____ • Other (list) _____ _____
3. Describe the Desired Performance		• Interviews (list individuals) _____ _____ _____

(continued on page 62)

Exercise 3-1. Needs analysis: six issues to consider (continued).

Needs Analysis Issue	Actions Required	Information Source(s)
3. Describe the Desired Performance (continued)	If the course is intended to address existing performance, describe that, too: _____ _____ _____	• Focus groups (list participants) _____ _____ _____
4. Identify Tasks in Expert Performance	Main task 1: Supporting tasks: • _____ • _____ • _____ Main task 2: Supporting tasks: • _____ • _____ • _____	• Interviews (list individuals) _____ _____ • Focus groups (list participants) _____ • A day in the life _____ • Documents (list them) _____
5. Describe the Learners and the Influences on Them (collect information on each key group of learners)	Demographics: _____ _____	• Interviews (list individuals) _____

5. Describe the Learners and the Influences on Them (collect information on each key group of learners) (continued)	Previous Knowledge: _____ _____ Influences: _____ _____ _____	• Focus groups (list participants) _____ _____ • A day in the life _____ • Documents (list them) _____ _____
6. Identify Constraints Affecting the Project	• Product constraints _____ • Technical constraints _____ • Business constraints _____ • Corporate culture, project history, and the learning environment _____ _____	• Interviews (list individuals) _____ • Focus groups (list participants) _____ • A day in the life _____ • Documents (list them) _____ _____

This chapter explored the issues that you need to investigate when beginning a training project. As mentioned at the beginning of this chapter, you also begin a training project by clarifying the objectives of the training program. The next chapter explores how to set those objectives—and how to assess whether learners have met those objectives.

4

The Basic
Instructional Objective

■ ■

What's Inside This Chapter

This chapter introduces you to the basics of writing measurable goals for a training program. These measurable goals are called *instructional objectives.* This chapter also explains how to write evaluation materials that assess whether a training program met its objectives. (Yes, you do this *before* you write the course materials.) Specifically, this chapter addresses the following:

▶ the basic value of objectives and evaluations
▶ the basics of writing objectives, or measurable goals, for a training program, which involves determining which content learners must master and distinguishing among main and supporting objectives
▶ general guidelines for evaluating a training program using the Kirkpatrick model for evaluating formal learning products, which involves preparing a satisfaction survey, a criterion-referenced evaluation, and follow-up evaluations.

In addition, a worksheet at the end of this chapter guides you through the process of preparing objectives and evaluations for your training program.

The Basic Value of Objectives and Evaluation

In the needs analysis, you learned about the sponsor's business needs, the desired performance, the tasks learners must master, who the learners are, and the constraints on the project. You're ready to begin designing the training program. Right?

Not quite.

Although you have identified the needs and determined what the training program should accomplish, you need to formally state the goals for it. By establishing these goals, both you and the sponsor have a common agreement about the purpose of the program.

Immediately after setting the goals—and before any work begins on the training program—draft the instruments used to assess whether the training program achieved these objectives. More specifically, draft the satisfaction surveys, tests, and follow-up surveys. If the objectives state what the course should do, then evaluations describe what successful achievement of those objectives looks like, as learning expert Robert Mager (1997) observed.

This chapter explains how to perform these activities. The first part explains how to write objectives—the formal statements of goals. The second part explains how to draft evaluations.

Basic Rule 15

Before beginning any formal work on a training program, you must do two things: First, formally state the objectives for the training program. Second, prepare the instrument, or test, that assesses whether the objectives have been achieved.

The Basics of Setting Objectives

Objectives are the goals that a training program must achieve. They state the content that the proposed training program must cover and the extent to which learners must master that material. Writing objectives is a widely followed practice among trainers. According to some studies, nearly 100 percent of all trainers prepare them as part of designing a training program.

Determining the Content that Learners Must Master

Two categories of information gathered in the needs analysis help you determine the content that you should cover in a training program. The first of these categories is the overall desired performance, which then becomes the overall goal for the program. The second category is the specific tasks learners must master to achieve the overall desired performance. The next section discusses this second category.

In terms of expressing the overall goal for the training program for the examples presented in the last chapter, you can define desired performance in the following ways.

New Sales School. Using relationship marketing techniques, new sales representatives (those with one or fewer years of experience) will sell all relevant products to their assigned customers, and generate follow-up sales from at least 50 percent of those customers within one year.

Notice how the term "new sales representative" is defined in a way that it can be externally verified. Also note that, although the original purpose of the course included properly completing forms, this dropped out of the overall purpose of the course so that the overall purpose could have a more singular focus. Furthermore, if sales representatives incorrectly process orders, they are not likely to have repeat customers. It is also noteworthy that the phrase "using their knowledge of the product line" does not appear in the statement of ideal performance. Sales representatives cannot sell relevant products unless they can match products from the entire product line with specific customer needs.

New Accounts Receivable Application. Users will process all accounts receivables using the new system, achieving self-sufficiency by June 15 (that is, requiring no more than 0.5 calls for assistance per month).

Notice how the term *self-sufficiency* is defined: "requiring no more than 0.5 calls for assistance per month." This objective can be externally measured and verified.

New Security Policy. By following proper labeling and security procedures, employees will not leak confidential material.

Notice the simplicity and clarity of the statement. When stating the ideal performance in the previous chapter, it included more activities than listed here.

Ultimately, however, activities like labeling information and locking it up merely represent a means to an end: no more leaks of confidential material. Furthermore, the additional activities outlined in chapter 3 cannot guarantee that material won't be leaked.

Writing Objectives

What specific content should be taught to achieve the overall desired performance? This is the second category of information needed when determining the content to cover in a training program. The list of tasks compiled in the needs analysis provides a good starting point for determining what should be taught. This list identifies the main tasks and supporting tasks that the training program must address, and it can help you start to write specific objectives for the program. As demonstrated in the examples just shown, you may adjust the tasks as you write the objectives. In fact, the process of writing objectives gives you a chance to reconsider the list of tasks and refine it.

Once you have a formal list of tasks, you can convert them to objectives. Objectives are written in a structured way, using terms that are both observable and measurable. *Observable* means that someone can visibly see evidence that the objective has been achieved. *Measurable* means that someone can assess the extent to which learners and businesses have achieved a specific objective.

Specifically, each objective should follow a three-part format, as shown in table 4-1.

The list of objectives usually emerges directly from the list of tasks identified in the needs analysis. If you wrote the tasks using action verbs, the objective is partly written. You would simply need to add conditions and the level of acceptable performance. You might also make sure that the action verb is the most precise one.

What makes an effective or ineffective objective? Consider these examples:

☑ *Know the procedures for installing WordPlus software.* This is not an example of an objective because it is not observable. You cannot see whether someone "knows" something.

☑ *Install WordPlus in five minutes with the use of instructions and without any errors.* This is an example of an objective. It is observable because you can see whether someone could install WordPlus in five minutes or less. It is measurable because you can measure the time needed to install the product and count the number of errors that occurred during installation.

Table 4-1. Writing three-part learning objectives.

First Part	Second Part	Third Part
An observable, measurable behavior: State this behavior using an action verb such as *install, type, describe,* or *state.* Avoid words like *know, understand, appreciate,* and *inform* for the tasks because knowing, understanding, and informing (and terms like them) cannot be measured. Usually, each task identified in the needs analysis becomes an objective (with alterations resulting from your review of this list).	*Conditions under which the task should be performed:* This part describes any situations that should be considered when measuring the goal, such as the availability of reference materials when users perform a task. Most frequently, the conditions state whether learners can have access to resources such as a textbook while performing the task.	*Level of acceptable performance:* This describes the extent to which the objective must be achieved to be considered complete, such as "without errors." The level of acceptable performance is assumed to be 100 percent, unless stated otherwise.
↓	↓	↓
"Label all documents classified as confidential with the word 'Confidential' in the top margin . . .	. . .using the automatic header and footer function of the word processor . . .	. . . with 100 percent accuracy (both in placing the warning and remembering to use it)."

☑ *Name the six key elements of a telecommunications system within 30 seconds and without the assistance of a manual.* This, too, is an example of an objective. The task is "name the six key elements." The conditions are "within 30 seconds" and "without the assistance of a manual." Because the level of performance is not stated, you may assume it is 100 percent.

☑ *Name the six features of WordPlus that distinguish it from other word processors within one minute and without any errors.* This is an example of an objective because the main task can be measured. "Within one minute" is an example of a condition, and "without any errors" indicates the desired level of performance.

In addition to ensuring that the action is stated concretely, other terms, too, might be open to several interpretations and must also be defined as precisely as possible. For example, suppose that the word *effective* is used. What's effective to one person might not be effective to another. Rather than use the word *effective*, state what is meant by the word.

Defining abstract words that are associated with privately held values in an observable and measurable way is called *operationalizing* a term.

Distinguishing Among Main and Supporting Objectives

As you distinguish a hierarchy of tasks in the needs analysis, you also distinguish a hierarchy of objectives when writing them. At the top of the hierarchy are the most important objectives that learners must master. These are called *main objectives* (a term that the author prefers to use because it is an understandable, plain-language term). In the instructional design community, these are called *terminal objectives* because these are the ones that learners must master by the time they terminate the course. A course typically covers between five and nine main objectives.

To master one main objective, learners must often master several subordinate ones, called *supporting objectives.* To master one of the supporting objectives, in turn, learners must sometimes master two or more *sub-supporting objectives.* In the instructional design community, supporting objectives are called *enabling objectives,* because they enable a learner to master the terminal objectives.

Figure 4-1 is an example of a partial hierarchy of objectives for the course on securing confidential data. Of course, you could simply develop a hierarchy in outline form rather than the flow chart shown in the figure.

Drafting the Evaluation

If the objectives state the goals of the course, the evaluation materials establish what successful achievement of those objectives looks like. For example, if the objective of a course is "no confidential data will be leaked," success would involve properly labeling confidential data to make sure people realize its sensitivity, and avoid inappropriate disclosure of the confidential data. The evaluation would present learners with data and ask them how they would handle it with an emphasis on making sure that confidential data is properly labeled and kept secure.

In other words, the evaluation presents a specific application of the content. By designing the evaluation in advance, course designers and developers can "teach to the test"; that is, design courses so that learners are most likely to achieve the objectives.

This section explains how to prepare evaluations. It first presents some basic issues underlying evaluation of training programs, and then explains how to prepare three types of evaluations.

Figure 4-1. Example of a hierarchy of objectives.

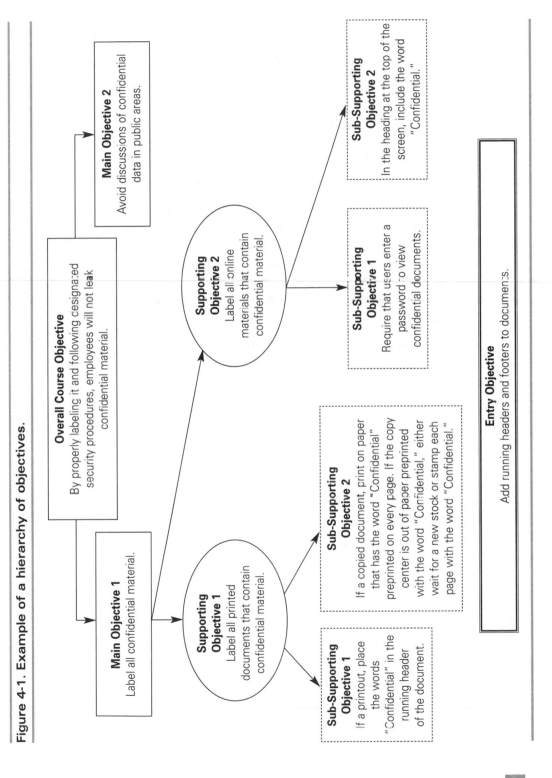

Overall Course Objective
By properly labeling it and following designated security procedures, employees will not leak confidential material.

Main Objective 2
Avoid discussions of confidential data in public areas.

Main Objective 1
Label all confidential material.

Supporting Objective 1
Label all printed documents that contain confidential material.

Supporting Objective 2
Label all online materials that contain confidential material.

Sub-Supporting Objective 1
If a printout, place the words "Confidential" in the running header of the document.

Sub-Supporting Objective 2
If a copied document, print on paper that has the word "Confidential" preprinted on every page. If the copy center is out of paper preprinted with the word "Confidential," either wait for a new stock or stamp each page with the word "Confidential."

Sub-Supporting Objective 1
Require that users enter a password to view confidential documents.

Sub-Supporting Objective 2
In the heading at the top of the screen, include the word "Confidential."

Entry Objective
Add running headers and footers to documents.

Think About This

In addition to writing instructional objectives, also consider writing a business objective for the training program. A business objective states the business goal in observable and measurable terms, much as the other course objectives describe the content in observable and measurable terms.

When you write a business objective, you include all three parts of an objective:

- *an observable, measurable goal:* The goal should focus on one of these three areas: generating revenue; reducing or eliminating expenses; or complying with governmental, industry, or corporate regulations.
- *conditions under which the goal should be achieved:* State the deadline when these business goals should be achieved, such as "within six months" or "by the end of the first quarter."
- *level of performance:* For goals pertaining to revenue or expenses, state the financial goal, such as "increase by 10 percent," or "reduced to 0.5% of sales."

Improving goodwill is not an example of a business objective. It is neither specific nor measurable. Similarly, containing support costs is not an example of a business objective. Which support costs? How much should they be contained? You must be more specific when declaring a business objective.

In contrast, meeting sales projections and reducing help line costs by 10 percent per user are examples of business objectives because they state specifically what types of business benefits should be achieved and how much improvement should occur.

Even if sponsors do not seem to notice these business objectives, write them anyway. First, they help you focus on the main goal of the project. Second, they educate your sponsor that training can achieve business goals.

Basic Issues of Evaluation

Trainers evaluate their courses for a variety of reasons. Among the most common:

▶ *to assess their own effectiveness:* Usually, this assessment is not as simple as whether or not a particular training program worked. It usually explores how specific parts of a program were received by learners on an emotional level, and how learners fared on assessments of their learning. Course designers and developers use this feedback to hone strategies that work, and rethink strategies that do not.

> ▶ *to assess whether learning occurred:* In some instances, only the learner uses this assessment. In other instances, management uses this assessment to determine whether or not a worker is eligible to do certain kinds of work or for determining eligibility for promotions. (For some promotions, workers must demonstrate that they have completed certain training programs.) There are also legal implications to the use of learning assessments, because they are used in making employment decisions. The test must be based on the content, and each learner who goes through the content should have an equal opportunity to pass the exam. Human resources and legal departments can provide you more details about the legal implications of testing.

> ▶ *to assess return-on-investment for the course:* Demonstrating how learners' performance improved provides a powerful tool in demonstrating the business value of courses because improved work performance can often be stated in financial terms.

To make sure that they provide useful data for making these assessments, evaluations must assess meaningful issues. In criterion-referenced evaluation, all test questions and other evaluations of performance are derived from the objectives, which are also called the *criteria*. Earlier, you determined the objectives: the content worth teaching. As a result, the objectives are the only content worth testing. In fact, the only valid evaluation questions are ones that directly emerge from the objectives. Other questions are ultimately gratuitous and irrelevant, and learners might perceive them to be trick questions.

Because one type of evaluation at one point in time provides incomplete data, trainers typically rely on several types of evaluations. In fact, the evaluations that trainers use come from the Kirkpatrick model, the widely used four-level framework for evaluating the actual and perceived effectiveness of training programs, which was described in chapter 1. As mentioned there, the different types of evaluations in Kirkpatrick's model assess participants' reactions to the program (level 1), how much participants learned (level 2), how much of the learning participants retain after a period of time (level 3), and the impact that the training program might have had on the bottom line of the organization (level 4). As mentioned in chapter 1, level 4 evaluations are beyond the scope of this book. Other books from ASTD can help you learn ways of conducting them.

Level 1: How to Assess Reaction

Almost every classroom course ends with a request for learners to complete an evaluation. Affectionately known as smile sheets within the industry, these surveys seemingly assess how much participants liked a course, whether the coffee was hot, the food fresh, and the instructor entertaining. Actually, these surveys can explore participants' reactions to much more substantive issues, including:

- ▶ whether they learned anything
- ▶ the likelihood that they'll apply the content
- ▶ effectiveness of particular instructional strategies
- ▶ effectiveness of the course "packaging."

The annotated example provided in figure 4-2 suggests questions to ask on a level 1 evaluation that can provide you with meaningful data about the perceived effectiveness of a course.

Level 2: Assessing Learning

A substantive method of assessing whether participants learned the designated content is by evaluating their command of the content immediately after completing the training program. Typically, this type of activity has been called testing, but because the term *testing* carries so much negative baggage, some learning specialists prefer to use the terms *evaluation* or *assessment*. The evaluation assesses whether someone learned something and, if the answer is yes, what the learner learned. If the learner did not master all of the content, the assessment identifies the specific content on which the learner should focus.

Assessing learning in a meaningful ways poses a variety of challenges, as described in table 4-2.

Consider the examples in table 4-3, which shows objectives and the test questions derived from them.

Think About This

The only appropriate test questions are the ones that emerge directly from the objectives. Although other questions and exercises might entertain learners because they do not directly relate to the objectives, they ultimately distract learners from the purpose at hand.

Figure 4-2. Example of a level 1 evaluation.

Your Opinions, Please

1. In a word, how would you describe this workshop? _____

Logic behind the question: Solicits open feedback about the course. Also lets you assess whether students accidentally transposed the numeric scales (if a student responds "Excellent" to this question, then circles "1" to the next question, chances are the student misread the number system.

2. Using a number, how would you describe this workshop?

1	2	3	4	5
Abysmal		Average		Outstanding

Logic behind the question: Provides quantitatively oriented organizations with the numbers they seek.

3. How much did you know about <SUBJECT NAME> *before* taking this workshop?

1	2	3	4	5
Nothing		Some		A lot

after?

1	2	3	4	5
Nothing		Some		A lot

Logic behind the question: Although this question does not assess actual learning, it does assess perceived learning. That is, do learners perceive that they learned something in the course?

4. How likely are you to use some or all of the skills taught in this workshop in your work:

1	2	3	4	5
Not at all		Not sure		Very likely

Logic behind the question: Determines whether learners perceived relevance of the course material. Perceived relevance is sometimes correlated with the satisfaction that learners feel with a course.

5. The best part of this workshop was: _____

_____

6. The one thing that could improve this workshop most is: _____

_____

Logic behind the last two questions: The last two questions provide qualitative feedback on the course and help prioritize work in a revision. Items mentioned by several participants warrant attention. For example, if 10 learners respond that the exercises are excellent, you should probably incorporate exercises like these in similar courses in the future. Similarly, if 18 learners comment that the pace of the course is slow, the pace should be quickened in the next revision.

Table 4-2. Some considerations for level 2 learning assessments.

Exactly when should the assessment be given?	Under ideal circumstances, participants would take an assessment before starting a training program to find out what they already know and then again immediately afterward. The difference between the scores of the "before" and "after" assessments is the true measure of learning. In the practical reality of everyday training, most organizations only conduct the "after" test, called a *posttest*.
What makes a good test question?	The only valid test questions emerge directly from the objectives. Because the objectives already suggest the task, questions are partially written.
	In practice, final assessments usually assess only the main objectives of the learning product. These assessments usually include one or more questions for each main objective. Because supporting objectives are ones that learners must master to successfully perform the main objective, explicitly testing main objectives implicitly tests the supporting objectives, as well. Within units, test questions usually assess supporting objectives.
	Rather than use test questions, some trainers give learners a scenario and ask them to address it. These trainers prepare a checklist indicating the main and supporting objectives that must be demonstrated while resolving the issue in the scenario.
How many test questions should be written?	To answer this, consider how many questions you might need for a given objective. In addition to a basic, end-of-learning-experience assessment, test questions can also be used for examples, which you work through with learners, exercises for learners to practice (sometimes more than one is needed), and reviews at the ends of units.
	On a single assessment, you might ask several questions about the same objective to make sure that the participant really learned the material and that the correct answer to a single question was not a fluke. Or, for security purposes, you might need to offer several versions of the assessment.
	As a result, you might need to write between three and 10 questions or scenarios for each main objective.
What kind of feedback should be provided?	The appropriate extent of feedback varies widely among situations.
	• In an assessment that will be used to determine whether a learner passes a formal course, instructors generally hold all feedback until the end so that knowledge of the learner's early performance does not interfere with later questions.
	• In an assessment primarily intended to help the learner assess his or her own learning, instructors generally provide feedback during the learning activity.

Table 4-3. Matching test questions to objectives.

Objective	Sample Test Questions
Match the countries with their capitals.	Match the country with its capital: a. France 1. Yaounde b. Cameroon 2. Brasilia c. Japan 3. Paris d. Thailand 4. Bangkok e. Brazil 5. Tokyo
Name the key steps in the instructional design process according to Dick & Carey.	Name the key steps in the instructional design process according to Dick & Carey. [Note that there's no change in wording from the objective.]
Describe at least three key benefits to small businesses of the X35 copier.	Martin Industries, which has 35 employees and $1.2m annual revenues, has decided to replace its copiers. Gina Loprieno, office manager, has invited you to make a presentation to the company in an effort to win the business. During the question-and-answer period, Gina comments, "This seems like a great copier but one that's better suited to a company that's much larger than ours. Why should we consider what seems to be more copier than we need?"
Using only the wordless instructions, install the desktop PC within 15 minutes and without errors.	You have just received a package containing a new desktop computer. Install it. You may use the instructions included in the box. (Instructor: Use this checklist when observing the performer and check off each box as the user performs it or indicate that the user did not perform the task.) ☐ Unpack the box. ☐ Identify components. ☐ Attach keyboard to system unit.
Using effectiveness criteria provided in class, recognize an effectively written performance plan.	On the following pages are samples of three performance plans. Indicate below which of the three are effective, according to the criteria discussed in class. (Instructor: You might develop an observation list to check off criteria mentioned in the response.)
Given a business case, evaluate the potential opportunity for e-commerce.	Read the following case. Afterward, evaluate the potential opportunity for e-commerce. Specifically name the criteria used in the evaluation. (Instructor: You might develop an observation list to check off criteria mentioned in the response. Leave room for criteria developed by the learner.)

Level 3: Assessing Transfer to the Job

The ultimate value of training is the application of its lessons to the job. Therefore, trainers like to assess the extent to which the content transfers into on-the-job behavior after some period of time has passed, also known as level 3 of the Kirkpatrick model.

In some ways, a level 3 evaluation is similar to a level 2 evaluation, in that it substantively assesses the learners' grasp of the content. The primary difference is that the level 3 evaluation is performed several weeks or months after the level 2 evaluation. The amount of time is at the discretion of the course developer, though the earliest that a level 3 evaluation should be conducted is six weeks and the latest is six months.

A variety of techniques are used to perform a level 3 evaluation. Two of the most common:

> ▶ *observation of the performance of tasks covered by the course objectives:* Such observation may occur either in the workplace or by computer "monitoring," by which a computer tracks each keystroke and analyzes it. The advantage is that the data is reliable because you have directly observed and collected it. The disadvantage is that, for human observation, the data requires extensive time to collect and analyze. Computer monitoring is not legal in all countries and may require a legal clearance before you can conduct it.

> ▶ *surveys of learners and their supervisors:* This evaluation method involves asking each learner and supervisor how well the learner can apply to the job the objectives (skills) taught in the training program. The advantage is that this is easily accomplished through email messages that are automatically generated and responses that are automatically tracked. The disadvantage is that the data is subjective. Because the data for each learner comes from two perspectives, however, it is more reliable than if the learner were the only respondent.

Getting It Done

Writing objectives first helps you focus the content of your training program and consider it in a hierarchy of importance (from desired performance to supporting objective). Writing test questions helps you maintain that focus, by providing a means for "teaching to the test." Use exercise 4-1 to help you develop the objectives and evaluation.

Exercise 4-1. Objectives and evaluations.

Business Objective (optional)	_____ _____ _____
Learning Objectives	Main objective of the course: _____ _____ Main Objective 1: _____ Supporting Objectives: • _____ • _____ • _____ • _____ • _____ Main Objective 2: _____ Supporting Objectives: • _____ • _____ • _____ • _____ • _____
Checking the Objectives	Make sure that each objective has: ☐ Observable and measurable behavior ☐ Conditions ☐ Level of acceptable performance (if other than 100 percent)

Evaluation	Have you prepared assessments of:
	• Level 1 (satisfaction)?
	  ☐ Yes ☐ No
	• Level 2 (learning, based on course objectives)?
	  ☐ Yes ☐ No
	• Level 3 (transfer, based on course objectives)?
	  ☐ Yes ☐ No
	Note: You can also prepare level 4 evaluations at this time, but a discussion of level 4 is beyond the scope of this book.

Now, try your hand at exercise 4-2. Some of its nine statements are properly worded objectives. Some are not. See if you can tell the difference. The answers follow the exercise.

Exercise 4-2. Recognizing properly written objectives.

Instructions: For each of the following, indicate whether it is a properly written objective.

1. Know the procedure for changing margins.	☐ Yes ☐ No
2. Understand the value of technical communication	☐ Yes ☐ No
3. Name four ways to assess the value of training products according to the Kirkpatrick model.	☐ Yes ☐ No
4. With the assistance of online help, change the margins on a page.	☐ Yes ☐ No
5. With the assistance of online help, change the margins according to a given request on a page 95 percent of the time.	☐ Yes ☐ No
6. With 80 percent accuracy, the five types of vertebrae in the spine.	☐ Yes ☐ No
7. Understand the key chemicals in the workplace.	☐ Yes ☐ No
8. With 85 percent accuracy and the availability of an online manual, employees should correctly complete an application for tuition reimbursement.	☐ Yes ☐ No
9. Customer service representatives should accurately update an employee record.	☐ Yes ☐ No

How did you do? Check your answers against these:

1. No. The task "know" is neither observable nor measurable.
2. No. The task "understand" is not observable or measurable. Similarly, the topic "value of technical communication" can be interpreted differently by different people, so it can be defined more precisely.
3. Yes. The assumed level of performance is 100 percent. Because no conditions are stated, none are assumed.
4. Yes. The behavior is change. The condition is with the assistance of online help. Because it is not stated, the level of acceptable performance is assumed to be 100 percent.
5. Yes, with a more precise level of acceptable performance.
6. No. No task is stated.
7. No, the task "understand" is not observable or measurable.
8. Yes. The task is "apply for tuition reimbursement." The condition is the "availability of an online manual." The level of acceptable performance is stated as 85 percent.
9. No. The term "accurately" is too vague and needs to be defined in more precise terms.

This chapter explained how to set the goals for a training program by writing objectives and preparing evaluations. The next chapter begins a five-chapter sequence that prepares you to design and develop your training program.

The Basics of
Organizing Courses

■ ■

What's Inside This Chapter

This chapter introduces you to the basics of organizing the content for a classroom or workbook-based course. Specifically this chapter addresses the following:

▶ Understanding the medium used to communicate the training content

▶ Organizing the content by providing a general structure for the course, considering the general structure of each unit, developing an overall structure for the specific learning content, breaking the content into units, planning for remediation and enrichment, and representing the structure with an information map.

In addition, a worksheet at the end of this chapter guides you through the process of organizing the content of your lesson.

Beginning the Design Process

With the needs identified, objectives formally stated, and evaluation in place, you can now begin designing and developing the course. (If you try designing and developing before completing these tasks, you might find yourself working on a course that has no purpose, whose audience is unidentified, about which different departments disagree on the intended outcomes, or similar calamities in waiting.)

This chapter begins a five-chapter sequence that walks you through the process of designing and developing training materials. It explores how to organize the content—the material covered in a course to fulfill its objectives. The chapter first describes the different communication media used in training courses. Next, it explores the general structure of all training courses and workbooks. Last, it offers suggestions for structuring the specific content of the course that you are developing.

Chapter 6 then explores a variety of ways to present content so that it engages learners and they retain the material. Chapter 7 explains how to develop course materials, such as student materials, slides, and instructor's notes for classroom and workbook-based courses. Chapter 8 describes guidelines for writing and designing these materials, and considerations for producing them. Chapter 9, the last chapter in the sequence, explains how to conduct reviews and pilot classes to ensure the accuracy and effectiveness of the materials before you make them widely available.

Media for Communicating Learning Content

The first issue to consider when designing a training course is the medium used to communicate the learning content. The discussion in this book thus far has not considered whether the course you are developing is intended for the classroom, a workbook, or some other medium, because you should analyze the needs underlying a course, write objectives, and develop draft evaluations before deciding how the material will be presented. As you design the course, the communication medium used to present the content is significant because you develop the learning content differently for a workbook than for the classroom or a computer.

In many instances, you are told which medium you should use when you receive the assignment. For example, a request might sound like one of these:

> ▶ The vice president of marketing and sales has requested a one-week classroom-based sales school and a series of workbooks to address prerequisite materials and postclass content. The sales school will be required of new sales

representatives and must cover relationship marketing, marketing policies, and ordering procedures, and it must provide an overview of the current product line.

▶ The manager of internal software applications has requested a half-day classroom-based training course for end users of the new accounts receivable application. The course must launch May 2, three weeks before the new application goes live.

▶ The chief security officer has requested a two-hour classroom-based training course for managers about the new security policy. The course must launch in eight weeks, when new security procedures begin.

A classroom-based course is one in which the learners and instructor are in the room at the same time. The room might be a traditional classroom, a corporate meeting room, a meeting room in a hotel or similar conference facility, an auditorium, or some similar gathering space.

Alternatives to the classroom do exist. One popular one is the workbook. As its name suggests, a *workbook* is a book that presents learning content. Learners go through the content at their own pace. Sometimes, the workbook represents the entire course. In other instances, the workbook covers prerequisite material, which learners must master to succeed in a later classroom course. Usually, organizations prepare the workbook with a desktop publishing system so that it has a professional appearance.

Note that a workbook-based course is one in which all of the material is in the workbooks. Sometimes, classroom courses have handouts that look like workbooks. But, workbooks provided as adjuncts in classroom courses are considered to be handouts, rather than workbook-based courses. The content in workbook-based courses stands alone.

Both approaches—classroom and workbooks—have advantages and disadvantages. A classroom course offers these advantages:

▶ It is among the easiest to develop.

▶ During the course, an instructor can easily adjust the learning content to the needs of the learners. If an instructor sees a puzzled look, the instructor can check for clarity. If a learner has a question, he or she can immediately ask it.

▶ Under the watchful eye of an instructor, a large percentage of learners complete the course.

Basic Rule 16

Although the original request to design and develop a training course might have identified the preferred medium, one of your first tasks must be to verify that the selected medium is the best one.

▶ Updating course content is easy, because it usually just requires a quick change of a slide or two, perhaps an update to an activity, and a change to the script.

The disadvantages of a classroom course include the following:

▶ Delivering the content is expensive because learners must leave their workplace to take training. Often, learners must travel, adding airfare, lodging, meals, and similar expenses to the total cost of the course. If learners do not need to travel, then instructors might. Additional expenses include rental or purchase of classroom facilities, equipment, and supplies for learners.

▶ Material is often presented inconsistently between sessions, because instructors adjust the material to the personality of each class. An instructor might use different words to explain a concept, introducing subtle differences in meanings, or cover material in one class session but not another.

▶ Learners have little scheduling convenience; they must take the course when the instructor offers it.

▶ With poor design, classroom sessions can degenerate into lectures.

Workbooks are an alternative to classroom training. These are some of the advantages of workbooks:

▶ Because the course is "portable," learners can take the workbook with them and learn at the time and place that is most convenient to them.

▶ The messages that learners receive when taking the same course at different times are consistent because each learner reads the same material in the same exact words.

▶ Other than printing and shipping costs, the cost to deliver workbook training is minimal. Travel expenses are not a factor in a workbook-based course.

Some of the disadvantages of workbooks are:

▶ Without the instructor's watchful eye or a similar type of support or incentive, fewer learners complete the courses.

▶ If learners have questions, they do not have an easy way to ask them unless a tutoring service is provided for workbook-based learners. Even then, learners cannot receive an immediate reply.

▶ Workbooks can be more costly to develop than classroom courses because they involve printing.

▶ Updating can be costly because all currently printed copies must be destroyed and reprinted. (If you only print workbooks on demand, you can avoid high updating costs.)

Think About This

Other media are also available for training. For example, computers can serve either as a *virtual classroom* (one in which the instructor broadcasts the course to learners who are in a variety of locations) or as a teaching tool (in which the computer presents content, provides exercises, and tests learners on their mastery of the material without a live instructor). This computer-based training is also called *e-learning* or *distance learning*. Another alternative is video, in the form of a television show (pretaped or live broadcast) that presents the learning content. Learning programs using only sound usually take the form of an audiotape or CD that presents the learning content and that learners listen to at their own convenience.

Because preparing learning material for computers, video, and audio requires specialized design and production skills that are beyond the scope of this book, and because they represent less than 30 percent of all training (at least, at the time this book is published), this book does not address them. Furthermore, when the design and development of classroom courses sometimes differs from that of workbooks, the discussion in this book will highlight these differences. One of the first places this becomes an issue is in organizing the content of a lesson.

The Basics of Organizing Content

Once you've selected the most effective training medium for the content you need to cover, you can turn your attention to organizing the content of the course.

Organizing content involves the following six steps, which are discussed in greater detail in the sections that follow:

1. Establish a general structure for the course, considering the elements that are part of every course but might not appear in a course outline. These elements include the administrative details at the beginning of a course, such as the agenda, and those at the end of a course, such as a list of related courses and the course evaluation.
2. Develop a general structure for each unit, considering elements that are part of every unit that might not appear in an outline, such as a title page and a unit summary.
3. Set up an overall structure for the specific learning content.
4. Divide the content into units.
5. Plan for remediation and enrichment.
6. Represent the structure with an information map.

1. Establish a General Structure for the Course

Every course and workbook follows a certain general structure, regardless of the content. Each begins with certain elements (called *front matter*), and ends with other elements (called *back matter*). Although these elements are supposed to appear in every course, unless you specifically plan for them, you might forget to include them.

Therefore, your first task in organizing the course is developing the general outline and making sure you include all of the front and back matter.

Front and Back Matter for a Classroom Course. The front matter for a classroom course includes the following:

▶ *title of the course:* usually a slide that identifies the course with the following information: (a) title of the course, (b) number or identifier of the course (such as HR-1544), (c) instructor's name, (d) department and organization that the instructor represents (such as Training Department, Acme Corporation), (e) copyright notice (see the description of the front matter for workbooks for an example of a copyright notice).

> *purpose of the course:* names the desired outcome of the course.
> *agenda or objectives:* a list of the topics covered by the course. The objectives are the main objectives of the course (and only them). (Supporting objectives are presented with the unit in which they are taught.) Some organizations use an agenda, some use objectives, some use both.
> *a review of prerequisites (if any).*
> *administrivia:* administrative information that orients learners to the classroom schedule and facilities. Administrivia usually includes (a) the time of breaks and meals, (b) the location of meals and breaks if they are provided, or restaurant suggestions (if meals are not provided), (c) the location of restrooms, (d) a request to turn off mobile phones, (e) emergency number, where learners can be reached in case of an emergency, (f) the location of emergency exits, and (g) other material, as suggested by your organization.

The back matter for a classroom course includes six items. First is a summary of the key points of the content. Second is a course exam or assessment, if one is offered. Third is a list of related courses and other resources. The fourth item in the back matter for a classroom course is information on how to receive follow-up support, such as Websites with additional exercises and material, a phone number for telephone support, and address for email support, if these are available. Fifth is course evaluation (and, if you offer it, information about a follow-up level 3 evaluation to be conducted several weeks or months after the course). The last item in the back matter for a classroom course is the certificate of completion, if you offer one (and, if you do not distribute certificates in class, information about how learners will receive them).

Front and Back Matter for a Workbook-Based Course. The front matter for a workbook-based course includes the following:

> *title page:* the first page of the course that provides the following information (a) title of the course, (b) number or identifier of the course (such as HR-1544), (c) instructor's name, (d) department and organization that the instructor represents (such as Training Department, Acme Corporation), and (e) date of the course.

▸ *edition notice:* contains legal notices, including the copyright notice. Here's an example of how a copyright notice should read:

© Copyright. ASTD. 2003. All rights reserved.

The edition notice also contains a list of trademarks, registered trademarks, and service marks used in the workbook.

▸ *preface:* introductory material that learners read to determine whether or not they should take the course. The preface includes (a) the purpose of course, which states the desired outcome of the course, (b) objectives—the main objectives of the course (not the supporting objectives, which are presented with the unit in which they are taught), (c) intended audience, which explicitly states the learners for whom the course is intended, (d) prerequisites, a list of the material that learners must have mastered to successfully complete the course, (e) instructions for taking the course, which describes how to take the course, unique symbols used in the workbook, and other information that might require an explanation before learners can effectively use the course.

The back matter for a workbook-based course includes six items. First is a summary of the key points of the content in the course. Second is a glossary (a list of terms used in the workbook). Third is a course exam or assessment, if one is offered. The fourth item

Noted

Many organizations have their own lists of items for the front matter and back matter (as well as instructions on how to prepare them). Before proceeding, check with your project manager to find out whether your organization has standard material for front and back matter.

Organizations that have their own lists of items for front and back matter often have templates—word processing forms that you can easily fill in to create these items. These templates not only simplify your work, but also ensure consistency among courses. If all course designers and developers use the same template for a preface in a workbook, for example, learners know where to find the information they need to determine whether a course meets their needs.

in the back matter for a workbook-based course is a list of related courses and other resources. Firth is a course evaluation (and, if you offer it, information about a follow-up level 3 evaluation to be conducted several weeks or months after the course). The last item in the back matter for a workbook-based course is information on how to receive a certificate of completion, if you offer one.

2. Develop a General Structure for Each Unit

In the same manner that each course and workbook has front and back matter, so each unit in a course or workbook has its own front and back matter. Like the front and back matter for a course, it is not uncommon to overlook the front and back matter for a unit if you do not take a few moments to explicitly identify it.

Front and Back Matter for a Unit of a Classroom Course. The front matter for a unit of a classroom course includes three items. First is a new unit slide, which indicates the title of the unit and its sequence (such as unit 1, unit 2, or unit 7). Second

are the objectives of the unit, which include the main objective(s) covered in the unit, and the supporting objectives. Last are the prerequisites for the unit, which identify the skills learners must have already mastered to successfully complete the unit. The list of prerequisites also indicates where learners can find this material (such as another unit or course), and might include a pretest to help learners determine whether or not they already have these skills.

Noted

Units go by a variety of names including unit, lesson, *and* section. *Use whichever term you prefer, so long as you use the same term consistently throughout the course (or, in cases in which your course relates to similar ones, all the related courses).*

The back matter for a unit of a classroom course includes the following:

- ▶ *descriptive summary:* states both the topics covered and the points learners should remember about them
- ▶ *assessment of learning:* an informal quiz or a formal test
- ▶ *resources:* where learners can find additional information about the topic
- ▶ *job aids and other resources:* materials that learners can use back on the job.

Front and Back Matter for a Unit of a Workbook-Based Course. The front matter for a unit of a workbook-based course includes three items. First is a title page for the unit, which usually begins on a right-hand page (easier to see when flipping through the workbook) and indicates the title of the unit and its sequence (such as unit 1, unit 2, or unit 7). Second are the objectives, which include the main objective(s) covered in the unit and the supporting objectives. Last are the prerequisites for the unit.

The back matter for a unit of a workbook-based course includes four items: a descriptive summary, an assessment of learning, a list of related resources, and job aids (and similar quick reference tools to help learners once they return to the job).

3. Set Up an Overall Structure for the Specific Learning Content

With the general outline of the course and individual units in mind, the next thing you must do is determine how to structure the content in the course and within individual units.

One large chunk of that work is already finished: the content (instructional) objectives. Only content that relates directly to the instructional objectives should be included in a course. Training professionals call this *criterion-referenced instruction,* because all instructional material emerges from the *criteria* (instructional objectives). These objectives state which content should be presented, the hierarchy of that content, and the order in which the points should be presented if learners go through the content in a linear fashion.

You can tie your objective-linked content together with an organizational scheme. Learners find organizational schemes helpful because they help learners relate one piece of content to another. Information architect Richard Saul Wurman (1989) suggests five general schemes—called hat racks—for structuring content. Wurman's five hat racks are

1. category (such as top 40, hard rock, rap, or classical music)
2. time (either a real chronological order, as in an account of an event, or an implied order, such as a procedure)
3. location (in reference to a place or a thing)
4. alphabet (as in a telephone directory, dictionary, or encyclopedia)
5. continuum (such as least to most, worst to first, and extreme conservative to extreme liberal).

You can develop complementary, though different, organizational schemes at each level of the hierarchy; that is, you can develop one organizational scheme for all of the main objectives and separate organizational schemes for the supporting objectives of main objective 1 and another for the supporting objectives of main objective 2. For example, if one part of a course addresses the types of security leaks, you might present them as a series of categories. If another part of a course presents procedures for securing information, you might present that information as a procedure (a time sequence).

4. Break the Content Into Units

After providing the entire body of learning content with an organizational scheme (and, in many instances, several layers of organizational schemes), you now need to break the content into small packages—the units.

By breaking the content into smaller pieces, you make it manageable for learners. As noted in chapter 1, adult learners have a limited attention span because they are pressed for time and because they have a finite capacity for content. Breaking the content into units helps control the quantity of information that learners must consider at any given time.

Although some would like to characterize the act of dividing the content into units as a science, the truth is, it's an art and, in some cases, you have to rely on gut feelings.

5. Plan for Remediation and Enrichment

Some learners do not grasp the material on the first try, other learners apply the material in a unique way, and still others will want to learn more about the topic. The best way to address all the learners' needs is to design with all of them in mind.

After you devise the general organization for the entire learning program and break the content into units, you should plan for three special needs of learners: remediation, special application of the material, and enrichment.

Remediation. Some learners need more assistance in learning than others; that is, they might not comprehend the material on the first try and might need to review it. This type of review—with the hope of correcting learning difficulties—is called

Think About This

Wondering how to divide content into individual units? Consider these guidelines:

- ☑ For a classroom course, a unit should last about 50 to 90 minutes (which, one experienced trainer said, is the longest a person can go between bio-breaks).
- ☑ For a workbook course, a unit should last no longer than 25 pages (including front and back matter for the unit). Assuming that learners need an average of two to three minutes to complete a page, 25 pages translates to 50 to 75 minutes of activity.
- ☑ In practical terms, each unit typically addresses one main objective. In the case of an extremely complex course, you might only cover one supporting objective in a unit.

remediation. When designing for remediation, identify material that learners might have difficulty grasping.

Next, identify those points where the learners' difficulties become apparent. This usually occurs after a quiz or exercise, in which learners have an opportunity to demonstrate their proficiency. At this point, plan for remediation—ongoing review of the content until learners master it. Some instructional designers have learners go through the material that was presented earlier. Because learners did not grasp it the first time, they are less likely to grasp it the second time. A more appropriate strategy is using an alternative presentation of the content. The presentation should assume that learners know less than was assumed in the basic presentation. It should also make use of other approaches, such as visual ones (if the previous presentation primarily relied on text). Also, begin the assessment with simpler practice questions.

Special Application of the Material. In some instances, a significant minority of the learners will use the content in a particular environment. For example, suppose that 30 percent of the learners taking a course on the corporate security policy work with especially sensitive material about new product information, whereas another 20 percent work with sensitive personnel data. Although both types of information are confidential, the reasons for keeping the material confidential, the means of protecting it, and liabilities for disclosing it differ.

In such situations, you can help learners make more effective use of the learning material by describing its application to the learners' environments. To do so, you would add passages to parts of the program that have specialized considerations. For example, in the unit about disclosing confidential material in public places, you might have two separate examples: one about the effects of sharing confidential product projections, another about sharing the particulars of an individual's family situation that is affecting that individual's work performance.

Enrichment. In some instances, some learners want to learn more about the content after completing a unit or course. If later units do not cover the additional material, you might support learners in their enthusiasm by providing links for enrichment.

Needs for enrichment vary, depending on the content and the learners. In some cases, enrichment might involve above-and-beyond exercises, ones that take learners beyond the content presented in the learning program. In other instances, enrichment consists of a listing of resources to help learners continue their learning: related learning programs (online and in the classroom), links to related Websites, and a bibliography.

6. Represent the Structure With an Information Map

After devising the structure for the learning program, record it. Although most people are trained to use outlines to represent the structure of a learning program, consider using information maps instead. As its name suggests, an information map is a diagram that shows the overall structure of a learning program. Because it shows how the content relates to one another, it is called a map.

Although not a standard practice, people who use them generally prefer information maps to outlines because the structure is more visible and easier to follow.

Generally, an information map has major nodes and minor nodes. Major nodes represent major sections of a learning program; minor nodes represent subsections. Figure 5-1 is an example of an information map for the lesson on corporate security. Notice that this information map only goes to the first level of depth (that is, it only covers supporting objectives, not sub-supporting objectives).

Getting It Done

Devising a format and structure for your course first involves verifying the choice of a communication medium (such as the classroom or a workbook).

Figure 5-1. Example of an information map.

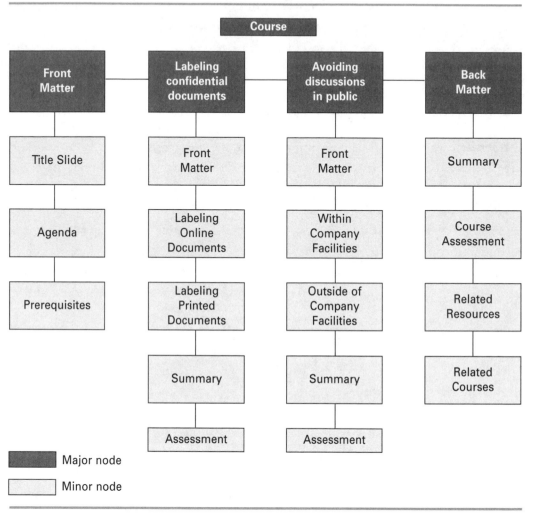

Then, you structure the content, which involves providing a general structure to the course, considering the general structure of each unit, developing an overall structure for the specific learning content, breaking the content into units, planning for remediation and enrichment, and representing the structure with an information map.

Use the following worksheet in exercise 5-1 to guide the effort of structuring the material for a course you are currently developing.

After you have chosen a medium of instruction and organized the content of your learning program, you can start thinking about how to present the material. The next chapter explores that issue.

Exercise 5-1. Organizing the content of your course.

Choosing a medium for the course	☐ Classroom (may include handouts) ☐ Workbook	
Establishing a general structure for your course	*For a classroom course, include the following:* **Front matter** ☐ Title page: ___ Title of the course ___ Number or identifier of the course ___ Instructor's name ___ Department and organization that the instructor represents ☐ Purpose: One of the following: ___ Agenda ___ Objectives (main only) ☐ Prerequisites (if any) ☐ Administrivia: ___ The time of breaks and meals ___ Location of meals and breaks ___ Location of restrooms ___ Request to turn off mobile phones ___ Emergency number ___ Location of emergency exits ___ Other material, as suggested by your organization **Back matter** ☐ Summary ☐ Course exam or assessment (if offered) ☐ List of related courses and other resources ☐ Follow-up support ☐ Course evaluation ☐ Certificates of completion	*For a workbook-based course, include the following:* **Front matter** ☐ Title page: ___ Title of the course ___ Number or identifier of the course ___ Instructor's name ___ Department and organization that the instructor represents ___ Date of the course ☐ Edition notice: ___ Copyright notice ___ List of trademarks ☐ Preface ___ Purpose ___ Objectives (main only) ___ Intended audience ___ Prerequisites (state as skills, not just names of courses) ___ Instructions for taking the course **Back matter** ☐ Summary ☐ Glossary ☐ Course exam or assessment (if offered) ☐ List of related courses and other resources ☐ Course evaluation ☐ Certificate of completion (if offered)

(continued on page 98)

Exercise 5-1. Organizing the content of your course (continued).

Setting up a general structure for each unit	**Front matter** ☐ New unit slide ☐ Objectives (the main and supporting objectives for the unit) **Back matter** ☐ Descriptive summary ☐ Assessment (such as a quiz or test) ☐ Resources ☐ Job aids	**Front matter** ☐ Title page for the unit ☐ Objectives (the main and supporting objectives for the unit) ☐ Prerequisites for the unit **Back matter** ☐ Descriptive summary ☐ Assessment of learning ☐ Resources ☐ Job aids
Developing a structure for specific learning content	Overall structure of the course: ☐ Category ☐ Time ☐ Location ☐ Alphabet ☐ Continuum ☐ *Structure for Unit 1:* ___ Category ___ Time ___ Location ___ Alphabet ___ Continuum	☐ *Structure for Unit 2:* ___ Category ___ Time ___ Location ___ Alphabet ___ Continuum
Dividing the content into units	Classroom courses: units should range from 50 to 90 minutes	Workbook-based courses: units should not exceed 25 pages

Planning for remediation and enrichment	• Plans for remediation: _____
	  _____
	
	• Plans for special application of the content: _____
	  _____
	
	• Plans for enrichment: _____
	  _____	

Representing the structure with an information map		

6

The Basic Strategies
for Presenting Content

■ ■

What's Inside This Chapter

This chapter introduces you to the basic toolbox of instructional techniques. Specifically, it helps you start to build your repertoire of course design techniques.

The chapter opens with a discussion of the characteristics of an effective learning environment—why presenting content involves more than imparting facts and building skills. Next, it presents these instructional strategies and explains how to choose an appropriate strategy for presenting specific content:

▶ Classical approach
▶ Mastery learning
▶ Discovery learning
▶ Hands-on exercises, or labs
▶ Performance without instruction
▶ Techniques for starting courses
▶ Techniques for ending courses
▶ Issues to consider when choosing an instructional strategy.

In addition, a worksheet at the end of this chapter guides you through the process of choosing an instructional technique, taking into account the practical considerations associated with that choice.

Characteristics of an Engaging Course

After you have chosen a communication medium for your course and organized the content, your next design challenge is planning the strategy for presenting the learning content.

For some course designers and developers, this is the most creative of the challenges because you choose among many different teaching strategies, or approaches, to presenting content. In some cases, the content seems to dictate the approach. In other cases, course designers and developers might see several workable strategies, and they must decide which one best fits with the particular set of learners and instructors involved.

More than creatively delivering the facts and developing the skills outlined in the objectives, choosing a presentation strategy means motivating learners to find meaning in the content and retain that content. So when choosing a presentation strategy, you also provide the foundation for a motivating, engaging learning experience.

Basic Rule 17

To make sure that learners want to learn and that the learning sticks, create a motivating, active, and supportive learning environment.

When learners want to learn and believe that they can succeed, they're more likely to do so. In fact, course designers and developers always keep this goal in mind when choosing a strategy. Specifically, they try to create a learning experience that is

- ▶ *motivating:* Before learners can master the learning content, they must feel a reason exists to learn it, and that they have the ability to do so.
- ▶ *active:* Learners learn best when they are actively involved in the learning experience. Course designers integrate activities into courses that actively engage learners in the learning process. In fact, some organizations require that a certain percentage of courses (say, a third of all material) involves active learning, such as exercises, case studies, discussions, and games.
- ▶ *supportive:* Learners learn best when they feel good about the learning experience. Therefore, course designers and developers design learning to enhance learners' feelings of success.

Noted

What makes content motivating? For some learners, certain content is intrinsically interesting. But that's just a small portion of the learners. For some learners, successfully mastering the content is essential to success in a new job or offers the possibility of career advancement, such as a better job assignment, certification, or a promotion. For other learners, learning new content means unlearning other content. As one designer for software courses commented,

> *Our learners often wonder why they have to learn a new system. They were satisfied with the old one. Management bought a new one without asking. The learners don't want to switch systems, much less learn the new one.*

In these cases, course designers and developers must address the barrier before any learning can begin. The more you uncover about learners in the needs assessment, the better you can identify these barriers, as well as motivators, to training and address them in your course designs.

Five Basic Strategies for Communicating Learning Content

Strategies for presenting content provide a framework for creating motivating, active, and supportive types of learning experiences. Each strategy motivates, involves, and supports learners in a unique way. The following sections describe five of the most common strategies used by course designers and developers:

- ▶ the classical approach
- ▶ mastery learning
- ▶ discovery learning
- ▶ hands-on exercises, or labs
- ▶ performance without instruction.

Some strategies involve more interactivity; others convey content more efficiently. Some are inexpensive to develop but involve little interaction; others require more

Basic Rule 18

Consider a variety of approaches to presenting content before making a decision.

resources but involve more creativity. No strategy is ideal. Each offers advantages and disadvantages for conveying your point. Consider how these advantages and disadvantages affect your particular learning situation before making a decision on how to communicate the content for learner. A discussion following the presentation of these strategies suggests ways to choose an appropriate strategy for presenting the content in your training program.

The Classical Approach

In a lesson designed according to the classical approach, the instructor broadcasts content to learners through a lecture. This is called the classical approach because it typifies the tradition of an expert transmitting content to learners. Some people refer to this approach as the "sage on the stage."

Noted

To maintain a supportive learning environment, you avoid overwhelming and embarrassing the learners. To avoid overwhelming learners, simplify the content. For example, if five ways exist to perform a particular task, present only one. To avoid embarrassing learners, start with simple exercises and work to more complex ones, so learners are always working at their comfort level. Similarly, only test content that has already been taught and that directly relates to the objectives.

In some cases, a lecture simply consists of an instructor speaking without interruption. More likely, lecture serves as the primary means of transmitting learning content, but the lecture is interrupted by a number of other learning activities. These might include screenings of videos and films, presentations by experts and other guest speakers, and classroom discussions resulting from questions posed by both the instructor and the learners.

The classical approach to training works best for content that must be transmitted as is, such as policies. For example, the content for the example course on how to apply the new security policy that was mentioned in earlier chapters might work well with the classical approach because learners must apply the content as is. The purpose of teaching is ensuring compliance with the policies, rather than just raising awareness of the issues.

One of the many advantages of the classical approach is that, when you approach it at its simplest, it requires few special resources such as equipment or special instructions. But, you do need to provide some support for instructors teaching in the classical mode. This support includes:

> ▶ For lectures, provide instructors with lecture notes that not only identify the key points to present, but also provide an additional level of depth with the content so that an instructor whose knowledge of a particular aspect of the topic is light can still effectively present the material.

> ▶ For discussions, provide discussion questions for the instructor, and anticipate common responses (both correct and incorrect ones, if it's that type of question) and how to respond to them.

Think About This

Typically, a lesson designed according to the classical approach contains this seven-step structure:

1. Gain learners' attention.
2. Present an overview of the content, including the learning objectives covered in the lesson.
3. Present the learning material through a lecture or with the assistance of a video or similar audiovisual program.
4. Discuss the learning material.
5. Provide practice problems.
6. Summarize the content.
7. Test learners.

> ▶ For guest speakers, be sure to provide the guest with the exact time and location of the presentation, the length of time available to speak, and an outline of the material you would like the guest to cover. Although some might believe that telling guest speakers what you would like to have covered interferes with their presentation, most presenters actually appreciate this guidance. It helps them target their comments and make the most effective use of class time.

> ▶ For videotapes and other audiovisual resources, provide instructions for using the equipment, state the frame number where the videotape should start (if you are not showing the entire videotape), note what learners should get from the videotape, and explain how the material on the videotape integrates into the rest of the learning content.

> ▶ For practice problems and tests, provide answer keys and points to discuss when reviewing answers (such as insights into why people might have made common errors).

Mastery Learning

In a lesson designed for mastery learning, the lesson begins with something to catch learners' attention. Next, the instructor describes and demonstrates a skill that learners must master to successfully perform their jobs. Then, learners practice the skill and continue doing so until they master it (hence, the name mastery learning).

One of the advantages of the mastery model is its straightforward approach to teaching: teach, demonstrate, practice. Mastery learning is popular for teaching technical skills to novices, especially when learners must perform those skills in a prescribed manner. For example, the mastery model is an ideal approach to teaching basic installation and troubleshooting procedures, and introductory word processing. The mastery model is also useful for teaching other types of skills, especially ones that require little or no interaction with other people, such as time management and manufacturing processes.

For example, mastery learning would work well for teaching end users how to use the new accounts receivable application mentioned earlier in this book.

Ensuring effective learning, especially during the demonstration and practice phases of instruction, requires that you provide extensive support to instructors. Instructors need a large number of exercises (as many as five to 10 for each concept taught) to provide enough practice opportunities should learners have difficulty mastering the material and need to practice several times. In addition, instructors need

Think About This

Typically, a lesson designed according to the mastery model follows a structure, which emerged from the work of Robert Gagne (1985), in which he suggests an ideal teaching sequence. The following list is adapted from his work:

1. Gain learners' attention.
2. Present an overview of the content, including the learning objectives covered in the lesson.
3. Explain the material.
4. Demonstrate the skill.
5. Let learners practice the skill with close supervision, providing positive or negative feedback at each juncture.
6. Allow learners to continue practicing the skill, reducing the amount of feedback until they can perform the skill without assistance. For example, learners might only receive feedback if they make an incorrect choice.
7. Summarize the content.
8. Test learners.

▶ instructions for administering the exercise problems

▶ information about correct responses to each problem

▶ background on incorrect responses that can be anticipated, so instructors can determine what learners misunderstood and correct that misunderstanding.

Discovery Learning

In a lesson designed for discovery learning, learners first encounter a problem that figuratively or literally places them in a real-world experience. By responding to the problem, learners "discover" key learning points. A debriefing that follows elicits and reinforces those learning points. The initial problem can take many forms, such as a simulation or case study. Because discovery learning allows learners to discover concepts by experiencing them, some people refer to it as a type of *experiential learning*.

Discovery learning is useful for teaching skills in which learners must make judgments. For example, the discovery model is popular for teaching management skills, of which decision making is an integral part. It is also useful for teaching advanced troubleshooting and customizing skills, especially for people who service and customize complex high-tech products in ways that go beyond existing documentation.

Think About This

The key challenge in choosing a problem for a discovery lesson is choosing one that richly represents the content to be addressed in the lesson, yet remains simple enough that a novice can address it. Note, too, that the problem should be a learning experience, not a trick. Among the possibilities you can consider are these:

• a case study, which presents the key issues underlying a problem and asks learners to identify issues that must be addressed by the solution, as well as suggest a solution

• a scenario, which presents a summarized version of a case (rather than a whole case) and ask learners either to identify the issues that must be addressed by the solution or, more often, indicate whether the way that someone handled the scenario was correct or not

• a simulation, which presents the key components of an environment and allows learners to interact with the environment and experience the benefits of good choices and the consequences of poor ones

• some other type of exercise to let learners experience the learning content.

Typically, a discovery learning experience typically follows this format:

1. a brief introduction, which presents the main learning objective covered by the lesson.

2. the problem, which can take many different forms (see Think About This on page 105).

3. debriefing of the problem, which is typically an interactive discussion of tangible lessons from the experience. This discussion is followed by an exploration of learners' feelings about the activity. The discussion concludes by abstracting key learning points from the exercise.

4. reinforcing the learning points by presenting them in more detail, with some additional support.

5. presenting a second learning problem (if needed) to give learners an opportunity to practice the skills.

6. summarizing the key learning points.

7. testing the learners.

Hands-on Exercises

Hands-on exercises, or labs, provide learners with an opportunity to practice skills with complex equipment and software. The labs might involve structured exercises with one correct solution and a limited number of correct ways of achieving it, such as courses that teach end users how to perform word processing or instruct hospital staff on how to use monitoring equipment. Or, the labs might involve unstructured exercises, with several possible paths to a correct solution, such as courses that teach service

Think About This

The heart of discovery learning experiences lies in the exercises. In the classroom, these exercises often follow paths that differ from the anticipated ones. Therefore, one of the challenges in designing a lesson following the discovery learning approach is developing the instructor's materials. As with exercises used in classical and mastery learning, the instructor's guide still provides guidance on responding to correct and incorrect approaches to exercises, and offers notes to assist instructors in leading classroom discussions. But, the materials also need to prepare the instructor to handle the unexpected.

representatives how to troubleshoot complex problems on telecommunications equipment or teach systems engineers how to configure complex computer systems. These labs are called *hands-on* because learners perform these tasks on real equipment.

Course designers and developers usually use hands-on exercises in conjunction with one of the three other approaches (classical, mastery, or discovery). That is, a course designer and developer might teach a course on animation software using a mastery model but incorporate hands-on labs to demonstrate how to use the software and give learners the opportunity to try it.

Before you can consider including a hands-on lab for use in a course, you must make sure that equipment will be available to learners during the course. For example, if learners are supposed to practice with brand-new software, you must receive assurances that the software will be available for use in the classroom. You must also

Think About This

Hands-on labs generally consist of:

- *purpose:* the learning objective(s) that the lab addresses.
- *instructions for performing the lab:* If learners have little or no experience with the equipment or software, then the instructions usually step learners through the process, one step at a time. If learners do have experience, the instructions generally identify the intended outcome and provide guidance for those tasks learners probably do not already know.
- *a description of the end result:* With software labs, this description might include a sample screen that shows "before" and "after." With tasks performed on equipment, the description might include a picture of the equipment after the task is completed, or the way that gauge should read on that equipment.
- *a description of anticipated problems and how to fix them:* When describing the problems, the description should describe what learners actually see or experience, not the cause of the problem. For example, suppose you are designing an exercise that gives learners an opportunity to change margins in a word processor. The exercise calls for learners to reduce the left margin from 1 inch to 0.75 inches, but the learner increases the margin to 1.25 inches. Rather than saying "margin error," your description of the error might say, "Your margin exceeds 0.75 inches." Then you might explain that the learner increased the margin when he or she intended to decrease it.

make sure that your learners will have access to systems that can run the software and that you will have enough systems available so each learner will have an opportunity to practice with them. Similarly, if learners are supposed to practice with a new piece of medical equipment, make sure that the equipment will be available for use in the classroom and that you will have a sufficient supply of that equipment so each learner can use it in a reasonable amount of time.

Because hands-on labs are almost always used in conjunction with other teaching models, a typical teaching sequence only covers the presentation and practice of the skill; it does not address broader teaching content. For example, a hands-on lab would give learners an opportunity to practice changing margins or adding a running header to a document. The plans for the lab would not explain why users would want to change margins or add running headers in the first place. That would be covered in another part of the lesson.

When preparing the instructor's materials for hands-on exercises, you also need to provide the following:

- ▶ instructions on how to introduce the activity, including the purpose of the lab, directions for the learners, and a demonstration activity (if needed)
- ▶ instruction sheets for the learners (including a copy for the instructor)
- ▶ a list of materials needed to run the activity (and, if appropriate, a copy of each material needed)
- ▶ an instructor's guide that lists for each step any anticipated problems and possible solutions for coaching learners through them
- ▶ sample files, if learners need to use material that is already stored in the computer
- ▶ accounts and passwords for students to use, so that learners can have access to content on the computer (if needed)
- ▶ a script for debriefing the activity, which starts with a review of the results and then offers suggestions for performing the task in an actual setting.

Performance Without Instruction

In some cases, learners can achieve the intended objectives without going through a formal training program. For example, rather than teaching learners how to calculate a complicated commission formula, learners might be able to calculate commission if you provide them with a coded spreadsheet. The spreadsheet can prompt learners to enter information about sales and—based on the product, special incentives in place, and agreements with the sales representative that are stored on the system—the spreadsheet would automatically calculate the commission.

In other cases, learners might need "smart forms" and reminders in their workplace of the information they learned in class to make sure that they apply the information on the job. For example, a programmer might have learned a number of commands in a training class, but he or she needs a quick reference to remember how to enter each specifically.

Resources like these that are intended to aid workers on the job are called *job aids*. Providing job aids and resources like these that go beyond training represent one of the options for presenting content to learners. Sometimes, you provide these resources in place of training if you have a high degree of confidence that workers will easily find the resource and use it when needed. In other instances, you provide job aids to supplement the training, providing learners with materials to help them easily apply concepts taught in class when they go back to the job.

Job aids have become nearly ubiquitous. You've probably seen laminated cards that serve as quick references. They are designed to fit into pockets so that workers can carry them around. Cash registers in fast-food restaurants have pictures of items ordered so cashiers do not need to remember prices. In offices, workers often create their own job aids, like the Post-it notes with handy shortcuts jotted on them. Because job aids stand on their own, you must design them so learners can use them correctly without any training or outside assistance.

Think About This

One of the challenges of designing learning activities is determining whether learners should perform them individually or work in groups with other learners. Each approach has its strengths and weaknesses. Hands-on labs usually involve tasks that learners must perform on their own in the real world on equipment and software that learners must eventually become comfortable with on their own. Providing each learner with an opportunity to practice on his or her own is helpful.

But, other exercises, especially ones involving problem solving, often require that learners consider a variety of viewpoints and seek outside opinions before solving the problem. Such problems often work better if learners work in groups. In fact, studies suggest that learning in groups often benefits learners.

Beginning and Ending Courses

Two of the most challenging parts of a course to design are the beginning and the ending, otherwise known as the "bookends." The beginning provides you with an opportunity to introduce the content and create a supportive learning environment. The ending provides you with an opportunity to remind learners of the key points they should recall, and motivate them to continue their learning of this subject. Going astray at either of these points can affect both learning and the motivation to continue learning.

The following sections offer suggestions for designing these two pivotal parts of a course.

Designing the Beginning of a Course

Like the first paragraph of a news story, the beginning of a course must grab the learners' interest, quickly summarize the points to follow, and relate the content of the course to the learners' needs. And, the beginning must do all these things efficiently—without taking too much time. In educational terms, the beginning of a course is called an *advance organizer*. Studies have correlated the presence of advance organizers with the effectiveness of learning. To provide an effective advance organizer to the content, course designers and developers try a number of strategies.

Noted

Some instructors start courses by asking each learner to introduce himself or herself, and explain why he or she wants to attend the course—bad idea! Although introductions may seem like a great way to foster networking, think carefully about using them. These introductions often take too long (as long as 30 minutes in a large class, about 10 percent of the class time in a one-day course) and end up demotivating the learners.

One design for an effective advance organizer for a classroom course is:

▶ Briefly introduce the purpose of the course.

▶ Ask those learners who choose to do so to state what they hope to accomplish by taking the course. This information lets the instructor gauge whether expectations will be met.

▶ To provide learners with an opportunity to network, begin with a group activity within the first 15 minutes of the course. Such an exercise efficiently lets learners network while immediately immersing them in the content of the course. The exercise might serve as a fun way to review prerequisite materials (if any exist) or pique learners' curiosity about the topic of the course.

▶ Use the debriefing of the exercise to introduce the main objectives of the course.

For example, consider figure 6-1, an exercise to start the course on security procedures. It presents the range of scenarios addressed by the course content while actively challenging learners to assess their presumed knowledge about the subject.

Designing the Ending of a Course

One of the most important parts of a course is its end. It is your last opportunity to reinforce the key learning points. Try to avoid an abrupt ending, that is, finishing the last unit and saying, "Well, that's it folks. Here's the postclass survey."

Rather, take a few moments to reflect on the content taught in class. Reflection differs from summarizing content, which you should do at the end of each unit. If you summarize content at the end of each unit, summarizing it at the end of the course seems repetitious. More important, the purpose of reinforcing the key points at the end of the course is not for the purpose of remembering content, it's to help learners integrate the content presented in the course into their own work. Reflection helps learners focus on integrating the content.

Figure 6-1. Example of an exercise for starting a course.

Instructions

1. Introduce yourself to the other members of your group.
2. Working in groups, determine whether the employee acted appropriately in the following scenario. If you cannot reach consensus, indicate so.

Scenario One

Michael, Jill, and Nicholas go to lunch in the employee cafeteria immediately after a heated meeting about their confidential new product. The point of contention in the meeting was the inclusion of three features in the product. The three of them debrief the meeting at lunch.

The employees:
- ☐ Acted appropriately
- ☐ Did not act appropriately
- ☐ Our group cannot reach consensus. Why?

Course designers and developers use a number of techniques to help learners reflect on the content. Here are some:

▶ providing learners with scenarios, asking them what they have learned in the class that specifically helps them respond to the scenarios.

▶ asking learners to state what lessons they will take away from the course.

▶ distributing preaddressed, stamped envelopes to learners and pieces of paper on which learners write some lesson or key points, place it in the envelope, address it to themselves, and seal it. The instructor mails the sealed envelope to learners at a specified time (one month to one year after the course). For example, the designer of a course on career development asked learners to list three things they should accomplish in six months, and then mailed them the reminder three months after class.

To make sure that learners recall the key points, most course designers and developers summarize them at the end of each unit. But how do you write an effective summary?

Descriptive summaries repeat the main highlights of a unit or course. In contrast, topic summaries only name the topics. Because the summary provides the last opportunity to remind learners of the key points, the summary must provide more than the names of the topics—it must provide the main points.

Consider again the course on new security procedures that was mentioned in previous chapters of this book. A topic summary of the unit on labeling content might read thus:

This lesson explained how to label confidential material. Specifically, it explored procedures for labeling printouts and online content.

Think About This

Two types of summaries exist. Topic summaries state the topics covered but give no details about them, and descriptive summaries state the topics covered as well as points that learners should remember about them.

Because the summary is the last opportunity to remind learners of the key learning points, always use a descriptive summary. A topic summary is too vague; it does not provide enough detail to promote recall.

Basic Rule 19

Always use descriptive summaries to recap content.

Notice how the topic summary only names the key points of the presentation; it does not tell learners what to remember. Learners who missed the earlier discussion must review their materials to find the main points, a great deal of work considering this is just a summary.

In contrast, consider this descriptive summary of the presentation on the new security procedures:

> Let's recap. This lesson explained how to label confidential material.
>
> When labeling printed material, place the word "Confidential" in the running header of each page of the document, using either the running header available with the word processor or printing the content on paper preprinted with the word "Confidential" on every page.
>
> When labeling online contents, use a two-level approach. Make sure that users must enter a password to see the confidential document. When the system displays it, make sure that the term "Confidential" appears at the top of the viewing area of the screen.

Notice how the descriptive summary provides key details that learners should remember. If learners happened to miss those points earlier, the descriptive summary gives learners one last chance to note them. They do not need to scroll back or interact with an e-coach to recall the main points.

Choosing an Instructional Strategy

Choosing an instructional strategy is part science, part art, and part hunch. In some instances, you choose a single strategy for the entire course. You sometimes do so because the course is brief and only requires one strategy. At other times, you do so because all of the material is similar in nature and, by choosing the same strategy for teaching it, you reinforce the relationships among the different units. In still other instances, when the material in each unit is sufficiently different that it benefits from a different approach to presentation, you choose different approaches for different units. Or, you might choose different approaches in different units to provide variety for the learners.

Choose a strategy that works for the content, the learning environment, and you. When choosing a strategy, you balance three needs:

1. *needs of the content:* Certain types of content lend themselves to certain types of presentation formats.
2. *realities of the learning environment:* Although some strategies might work better for the content than others, they might require resources that are not available. For example, simulations are great, but often require extra time to develop—time that many tight schedules do not permit.
3. *your preferences:* Most course designers and developers tend to rely on a limited number of strategies because they have had the most success with them.

Your choice of a learning strategy ultimately reflects a balance among these three needs.

Also note that you might need to alter your plans if the practical realities of the classroom limit your ability to effectively use a strategy. For example, suppose that a course designer and developer wanted to include hands-on exercises that let learners print the word "Confidential" in the running header of each page of a course workbook. Later, the course designer and developer learns that the classroom where the course will be taught does not have computers for students to use and is not likely to get them. The course designer and developer must change the instructional strategy to match the practical realities of the classroom. Rather than a hands-on exercise, the course designer and developer might choose instead to demonstrate this skill as a part of the lecture (classical model).

In the end, the strategy that you choose is the one that you feel will work most effectively in a given learning context and that you feel comfortable using. One of the challenges is that some course designers and developers only feel comfortable using a limited number of instructional strategies, and their courses start to seem monotonous after a while. The strategies that course designers and developers use most frequently are called their *repertoire* or their *bag of tricks*. The more strategies that a course designer and developer can integrate into a classroom experience, the more varied the learning experience.

Getting It Done

Choosing a strategy for presenting the content begins with some general considerations for creating a motivating, active, and supportive learning environment. Then, you determine how to present the content in each section. You choose a general instructional strategy, such as classical, mastery, discovery, hands-on labs, or performance without instruction. You also determine how to begin and end the unit.

Use exercise 6-1 to guide you through the decisions made in presenting the content. It provides a checklist of issues you might address as you design the presentation.

Exercise 6-1. Selecting an instructional strategy.

Making a Choice

For each unit, determine which of the following instructional strategies you plan to use:

- ☐ The classical approach
- ☐ Mastery learning
- ☐ Discovery learning
- ☐ Hands-on exercises
- ☐ Performance without instruction

Checking Your Design

For units following the classical approach, make sure that they:

- ☐ Identify the learning objectives
- ☐ Provide an outline of the discussion
- ☐ Anticipate questions that might arise and identify points to include in responses

For units following the mastery learning approach, make sure that they:

- ☐ Provide material so instructors can demonstrate
- ☐ Provide a sufficient number of exercises so learners can master the content
- ☐ Provide the correct response and anticipated errors for each exercise (either wrong answers or errors that might arise as learners perform the activity)

For units following the discovery learning approach, make sure that they:

- ☐ Provide a meaningful exercise that directly relates to the objectives and suggests how learners might apply the concepts in their work
- ☐ Provide an outline for the debriefing

(continued on page 116)

Exercise 6-1. Selecting an instructional strategy (continued).

For units following hands-on exercises, make sure that:

☐ Equipment and software is available

☐ Enough copies of the equipment and software are available

☐ Labs include:

___ Instructions on how to introduce the activity

___ Instructions for learners

___ A list of anticipated problems that might arise during the exercise and suggestions on how to coach learners around those problems

___ Sample files and accounts on the computer

___ Outline for a debriefing of the learning activity

For units promoting performance without training, make sure that learners can use them:

☐ Without training

☐ Without assistance

Thinking About Other Design Issues:

When starting courses, have you provided learners with an opportunity to state what they hope to accomplish in the course?

☐ Yes ☐ No

When starting courses, have you provided an exercise that actively engages learners within the first 15 minutes of the course?

☐ Yes ☐ No

When ending courses, have you provided learners with an opportunity to reflect on how they plan to integrate the content?

☐ Yes ☐ No

When ending units, have you provided a descriptive summary rather than a topic summary?

☐ Yes ☐ No

This chapter introduced you to instructional strategies and how to choose among them. Chapter 7 identifies the specific materials you need to prepare when developing a classroom or workbook-based course.

7

The Basics of Developing Course Materials

▪ ▪

What's Inside This Chapter

This chapter explains how to develop the materials used in classroom and workbook-based courses. Specifically this chapter explains the following:

▶ The basics of preparing the student's and instructor's guides for the classroom
▶ The basics of preparing workbooks.

In addition, a worksheet at the end of this chapter identifies the materials you need to prepare for classroom and workbook-based courses. Finally, note that this chapter focuses exclusively on choosing the content for these materials. Chapter 8 explains how to design, write, and produce the learning materials.

Getting Started

After determining how you plan to present the content, you can start developing the course materials. The specific materials that you prepare vary, depending on whether you are developing a classroom or workbook-based course:

▶ For classroom courses, you develop two sets of materials: a basic set for learners and an annotated set for instructors.

▶ For workbook-based courses, you develop a student workbook. In some cases, it is self-contained. In other instances, you develop an annotated version for a tutor.

This chapter explains how to prepare the content required for both types of courses. First, it identifies the types of materials you'll need for each type of course, and then it identifies the material you need to develop for specific types of learning activities such as lectures and case studies. Chapter 8 continues this discussion by explaining how to design, write, and produce the learning materials.

The Basics of Preparing Materials for the Classroom

When preparing for a classroom course, you prepare two general categories of materials:

▶ the student's guide, which usually consists of a copy of all the visuals in the course, exercises, and supplemental information (such as relevant articles, fact sheets, and job aids).

Noted

Although this chapter focuses almost exclusively on the type of instructions and materials you need to provide as you develop the course, you should always make sure that the specific content in those materials relates directly to the objectives. Learning activities that do not directly address one or more objectives distract learners from the ultimate goal of the course. In other words, if you have a great case study to present but it does not directly relate to the objectives, choose another learning activity because this case study won't help learners achieve the objectives.

▶ the instructor's guide, which usually includes an annotated copy of the visuals in the course. These notes suggest what the instructor should say during a lecture. The instructor's guide also contains annotated instructions for exercises, including instructions for setting up the exercise, administering the exercise and conducting the debriefing, in addition to a copy of the materials provided to learners.

The following sections explain how to produce the student's and instructor's guides. The explanation of how to produce a student's guide covers how to prepare visuals, exercises, and supplemental information. The discussion of how to prepare an instructor's guide covers setup instructions, annotated visuals for lectures, and instructions for administering learning activities. The discussion of administering learning activities has separate sections for administering general discussions, case studies, hands-on exercises, and instructional games.

Preparing the Basic Student's Guide

The student guide provides learners with the materials they need to complete the course. These materials include

- the visuals, which provide a record of the conversation in the classroom
- materials needed to complete the exercises
- supplemental information that learners might use in exercises, on the job, or both.

Basic Rule 20

A student guide is a self-contained package that learners use both in class and as a reference on the job.

Preparing Visuals. The backbone of nearly every corporate training course is its visuals. Visuals are slides or overhead transparencies that convey the key points of the course. For learners, visuals

- provide a record of key words that learners can follow during the class. These key words help learners reconnect with the conversation when their attention lapses (a likely situation because learners can listen three or four times faster than an instructor can speak).
- present a visual hierarchy of points, so learners can see the relationship among different points.
- convey key points visually (for example, a picture of a page marked "Confidential" on a slide shows learners in a course on company security policies exactly how to identify confidential material in printed documents).

Basic Rule 21

Visuals serve as a reminder, not a script of the class. Therefore, watch the amount of content placed on them.

In other words, visuals emphasize key points and supplement classroom activity. Although they do not serve as a transcript of the course, visuals represent the closest thing to one, so learners like to have copies of the visuals as a reference when they return to the job.

When determining which medium to use for your visuals and what content to include on the visuals for a training course, you need to consider several issues. The first is whether to use slides or overhead transparencies.

Because computers have become the preferred means of projecting visuals, slides are the most common style of visuals used in corporate training. In some instances, however, trainers choose to use overhead transparencies. Some instructors prefer transparencies because equipment for projecting images from a computer is not available to them. In other cases, instructors actually do prepare a set of visuals, but also prepare a set of transparencies as a backup, should computer problems arise.

Noted

Though the term slide is used in this book, the guidelines refer to both slides and transparencies unless they specifically mention the term transparencies.

Visually, slides and transparencies differ in two ways. First, slides have a horizontal orientation (3 units high by 5 units wide). In contrast, transparencies have a vertical orientation (11 units high by 8.5 units wide). The second difference is that slides generally have dark backgrounds and transparencies generally have light (clear) backgrounds. The next several paragraphs provide specific guidelines for preparing slides.

A typical slide has a standard structure, as shown in figure 7-1. Notice the two main parts of the slide: the heading and the content area. The heading is an area that contains between three and five words, identifying the purpose of the slide. The content area contains key words that convey the purpose of the slide, often presented as bullet points, and visuals. Content might consist of words, visuals, or both.

Figure 7-1. Standard structure of a slide.

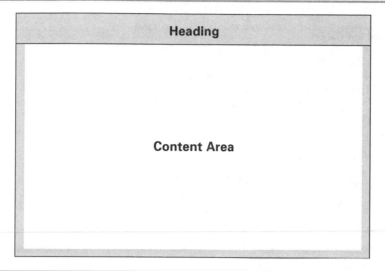

Although slides provide a record of the conversation in class, they are not a transcript of the lecture. As mentioned, they only contain key words. Experts in speech-communication therefore recommend the following guidelines:

- Limit the total number of words on any given slide to 35 (including the heading).
- Limit headings to five words.
- Limit the number of bullet points to five per slide. If needed, you may go up to seven, but try not to exceed that number. More than seven bullet points overwhelms learners.
- Limit each bullet point to seven words.

How many slides will the instructor need? Until someone actually presents them in a classroom, there's no way to know exactly how many slides an instructor will have time to go through in a class. However, you can use past experience and the experience of other instructors to estimate an appropriate number of slides for a course (table 7-1). Some general guidelines are discussed in the following sections.

Chapter 8 continues the discussion of preparing slides, by offering suggestions for designing slides and editing the content on them.

Table 7-1. Determining the number of slides to use.

If the Course Is:	Plan for:	Estimated Total Number of Slides
Less than 8 minutes total	1 slide per minute	8 or fewer
8 to 30 minutes	Approximately one slide for every 3 minutes	4 to 10
30 to 90 minutes	Approximately one slide for every 3 to 5 minutes	6 to 30
More than 90 minutes	Approximately one slide for every 8 to 10 minutes (this includes time for class discussions and activities, which often do not involve slides)	10 or more

Preparing Exercises and Supplemental Information. In this part of the student guide, you first provide learners with the information they need to complete exercises and other learning activities, then offer supplemental information that learners might find useful on the job.

To complete exercises and other learning activities, learners need some materials and information:

▶ State the purpose of the activity through a clearly worded heading.

▶ For case studies and similar exercises, learners need (1) instructions for reviewing the case; (2) the case or similar background information on which learners base their responses; and (3) questions to respond to, forms to complete, or similar types of material for responding to the case.

▶ For hands-on exercises, provide (1) passwords, user IDs, and similar information needed to gain access to the equipment or software; (2) step-by-step instructions for completing the activity; (3) hints for working past known trouble spots; (4) illustrations showing what successful completion looks like; and (5) illustrations showing known incorrect solutions and what caused them.

Figure 7-2 shows an example of an exercise for a management training course.

Figure 7-2. Example of an exercise.

Exercise 1: Hiring Discussion

Instructions:

1. Read the following scenarios.
2. Indicate whether the manager handled the situation appropriately or inappropriately.

(And, as the business world requires that managers make decisions so you, too, must choose one of the alternatives listed.)

What the Manager Did:	These Actions Were (Choose One, No Fair Saying "I Don't Know"):	
Bill manages one of five technical communication departments at the development lab for a major software manufacturer. Bill's lab is in a smaller community (about 50,000 people), two hours from the nearest major metropolitan area. While speaking to a class of seniors in the technical communication program at a major university in a major metropolitan area, Bill responded as follows to a student question about SGML: "Well, if you don't know it, we wouldn't even consider hiring you."	☐ Appropriate	☐ Inappropriate
Phyllis manages a documentation department of 10 women, mostly over age 40, and two men. She recently gave a second interview to Rich, a brash 24-year-old. He's very qualified for the job and Jessica, the lead writer he would work most closely with, seems to think he'd work well. But Phyllis found Rich to be a bit pushy in the interview and decides not to hire him, because she's afraid she'd be managing too much "broken glass."	☐ Appropriate	☐ Inappropriate

Supplemental information provides learners with materials that they might find useful back on the job. In some instances, learners also use this material in class.

What should you provide in the way of supplemental materials? Although the exact supplemental material varies, table 7-2 suggests materials that learners might find helpful.

Assembling the Student Guide. After you've prepared the visuals, exercises, and supplemental materials, assemble them into a single "package," comprising the student

Table 7-2. Supplemental material to provide learners.

For This Type of Training:	Provide This Supplemental Information:
Product Training	• Product information, such as brochures and fact sheets • Testimonials from customers who participated in trials • Technical articles by product engineers and programmers (after receiving permission to publish any copyrighted material) • For training service representatives, include reference material that they might need to complete exercises in class, such as quick reference sheets that list information widely used in the job
Marketing Training	• Articles about sales techniques and your product line from marketing magazines (after receiving permission to re-publish any copyrighted material) • Quick reference material about products
Management Development	• Copies of corporate policies • Copies of forms (when needed) • Articles about management issues from corporate newsletters and magazines to popular press (after receiving permission to re-publish any copyrighted material)
Medical Training	• Product information, such as brochures and fact sheets • Testimonials from customers who participated in trials • Technical articles by medical staff and product engineers (after receiving permission to re-publish any copyrighted material) • Other relevant articles from the scientific and trade press (request permission to reprint these, too) • For training service representatives, include reference material that they might need to complete exercises in class
New Employee Orientation	• Copy of the employee handbook (if your organization has one) • Information about employee benefits (if not already distributed to them) • Information about the company's products, services, and history
Manufacturing Training	• Reference material that the staff needs while performing manufacturing processes • Information about the product staff is assembling
Safety Training	• Signs, warnings, and similar job aids to post in the workplace to remind learners about safety on the job

guide. Usually you assemble these materials using your word processor or desktop publishing program. A typical student guide follows this structure:

1. title page
2. table of contents (most word processors will automatically produce this; see the next chapter for information on how)
3. edition notice (page with copyright statements)
4. visuals
5. exercises
6. supplemental information
7. references and other sources of information
8. evaluation form.

In many cases, some or all of the supplemental materials come from other, already published, sources. In such situations, you might not reprint them in the student guide. Instead, the instructor would separately distribute these materials in class.

Preparing the Basic Instructor's Guide

The instructor's guide provides annotated versions of the visuals; the annotations help the instructor lead class sessions. The guide also provides annotated versions of the exercises, which not only provide hints the instructor can give to help learners complete activities, but also information to help the instructor complete the debriefing of activities. In general, you do not annotate supplemental materials provided to learners.

Specifically, an instructor's guide contains (1) setup instructions, (2) annotated visuals to use in lectures, (3) instructions for administering learning activities, and (4) a close-out list for ending the course. The following sections explain how to prepare each of these.

Setup Instructions. These instructions serve as a to-do list for preparing for a class session. Specifically, the instructions provide instructors with a list of materials needed to

Basic Rule 22

Include all of the materials needed to administer the course in an instructor's guide.

run the class, including materials needed for demonstrations and learning activities, software and files used in the course, and other materials as needed. They also tell instructors where to find these materials.

Annotated Visuals for Lectures. The annotated visuals include notes that guide the instructor through the discussion associated with that slide. Figure 7-3 shows an example of an annotated slide.

Figure 7-3. Example of an annotated slide.

Review Incentives

- **Salary and benefits**
- **Signing bonuses**
- **Additional vacation**
- **Training**

NOTES

Review incentives: The entire offer package matters, not just the bottom-line salary.

Salary and benefits: Salary might be competitive but also need to see how benefits stack up. Medical co-pays? Flex time? Family leave?

Signing bonuses: Have been popular. Way of making up for a lower salary without raising base salary.

Additional vacation: Especially useful for experienced workers, who are concerned about losing accrued vacation time by jumping to another company.

Training: Studies suggest that the ability to develop new skills attracts new workers. One way of demonstrating this commitment is the amount of training promised.

Anticipated questions:
My company is not willing to review these. What can I do?
Response: Document cases when your first-choice candidate specifically rejected your offer because of one of these issues and build a case for HR to review organizational policies.

Most course designers and developers provide notes for each bullet point on a slide, but avoid a word-for-word script because instructors are not likely to memorize it. More significantly, if they rely on a word-for-word script, instructors may feel reluctant to add material from their own experiences. In addition to notes for each bullet, also list questions that are likely to arise during the lecture and suggest responses.

Noted

If you use presentation software such as Microsoft PowerPoint or Lotus Freelance, you can annotate the slides as you create them. You do so by using the "notes" view of the slide. The screen has a location specifically labeled "notes" where you type this information.

Instructions for Administering Learning Activities. For learning activities, instructors usually need significantly more information than learners do. For example, to start an activity, instructors often need instructions on how to prepare for the activity and introduce the activity to learners.

For example, consider these instructions for starting a case study activity:

First, point out the page number of the activity in the student guide. Second, divide the learners into teams of approximately five people. Then, give learners about 15 minutes to discuss the case.

When running the activity, instructors need information on how to resolve anticipated problems that might arise, the solution, and anticipated wrong responses—and how to fix them.

When concluding the activity, instructors need a guide for running the debriefing discussion. Figure 7-4 shows an example of the instructor's guide for a debriefing of a case study activity.

The specific way that you approach the administration of learning activities varies, depending on the type of activity being administered. Table 7-3 provides some guidance on the types of materials needed for four common instructional activities: general discussions, case studies, hands-on exercises, and instructional games.

Close-Out List. This section describes any activities that the instructor must perform to finish the class. These might include grading tests (if required), returning materials (if required), and conducting a follow-up with learners (if requested).

Figure 7-4. Example of a guide for a postclass discussion.

Debriefing Bill

Case: Bill manages one of five technical communication departments at the development lab for a major software manufacturer. Bill's lab is in a smaller community (about 50,000 people), two hours from the nearest major metropolitan area. While speaking to a class of seniors in the technical communication program at a major university in a major metropolitan area, Bill responded as follows to a student question about SGML: "Well, if you don't know it, we wouldn't even consider hiring you."

1. Ask people to raise their hands if they thought Bill's actions were appropriate. Then ask people to raise their hands if they thought Bill's actions were inappropriate.

2. Ask people who thought the actions were appropriate to explain why.

   Anticipated responses: These are the skills we need on the job. One needs to be clear about expectations, starting with the hiring process.

3. Ask people who thought the actions were inappropriate to explain why.

   Anticipated responses: Skills are secondary to the job. Will scare off good candidates who don't have these skills. Recruiting young people in large metropolitan areas to take jobs in smaller communities is a challenge.

Learning Points

- Admit that learners do not have the entire picture. Tight competition exists for the students graduating from this program.
- Note that the real skill that Bill seeks is communication skills; SGML is a tool needed to complete the job.
- Unnecessarily requiring such technical skills was popular when skilled labor was more plentiful.
- But, by hiring for software skills over other the real ones needed to complete the job, Bill might be discounting otherwise qualified candidates.
- Before going into the hiring process, review the job qualifications to make sure that the job description you write attracts the kinds of candidates who will really meet your needs (the objective of the unit).

Table 7-3. Administering learning activities.

	Introducing the Activity	Running the Activity	Managing the Post-Activity Debriefing
General Discussions	Explain how the learning activity relates to the objectives.	• Provide discussion questions. • Anticipate responses from students, and include them in the instructor's guides. • Suggest replies to different anticipated responses.	Label and reinforce the learning points. With these points identified, they can be presented in more detail with additional support. For example, if the discussion explored approaches to handling a discipline problem in the workplace, this part of the debriefing might present the most common strategies for addressing behavior problems and corporate policies regarding persistent behavior problems. These materials might also be part of the visuals.
Case Studies	• Explain how the learning activity relates to the objectives. • Point out the location of guiding questions that learners should answer (if any). • State the form of the response (if a particular format is required).	• Give copy of the case study to learners. • Divide learners into discussion groups to review the case (if needed).	• Provide solution to the case (often not distributed to learners). • Provide a discussion guide for the debriefing that addresses the following points in this order: (1) Discuss tangible experiences from the experience; (2) explore learners' feelings about the activity and the learning experience; (3) identify the key learning points from the exercise; (4) label and reinforce these learning points. With the points identified, they can be presented in more detail, with material to support them. For example, the case might have explored business strategy. This part of the debriefing might name three principles to consider when planning a business strategy. The discussion points might also be part of the visuals.

(continued on page 130)

Table 7-3. Administering learning activities (continued).

	Introducing the Activity	Running the Activity	Managing the Post-Activity Debriefing
Hands-on Exercises	• Describe the purpose of the lab. In addition to explaining the overall purpose of the exercise, these instructions should explain how the exercise fits into the goal of the course, and the objectives of the unit in which it is included. • Provide instructions for performing the lab. • Demonstrate activity, if that is needed. • Divide learners into groups, if needed.	• Provide a copy of the instruction sheets given to learners. • For each step in the instructions given to learners, provide the instructor with a list of anticipated problems and suggest how to coach learners around those problems. • Provide sample files if learners need to use material that is already stored in the computer. • Arrange for accounts and passwords for students to use so that learners can access content on the computer. Most of these accounts have limited access to other resources so that learners cannot gain access to confidential information and so that learners cannot work with active files and possibly affect the ongoing work of the organization. For example, if learners are taking a course on a new accounts receivable application, you would have installed sample files on the computer with the names of "dummy" customers. If learners make mistakes, these mistakes will not affect the accounts of real customers. Or, if a learner finishes early and gets bored, he or she cannot gain access to this information.	• Review the results, including a visual example of a successfully completed project. • Ask learners what they did—where they went right and where they went wrong. • Offer suggestions for performing the task in an actual setting.

| Instructional Games | • Explain how the learning activity relates to the objectives.
• Provide instructions for performing the game.
• Divide participants into groups (if needed). | • Provide annotated instructions given to learners. The notes should identify known problem areas and offer suggestions that the instructor can give to learners for working past the problems.
• Provide game materials such as a board, card, dice, and playing pieces, as needed. | Discussion guide for the debriefing should address the following points, in this order:
• Discuss tangible experiences from the game.
• Explore learners' feelings about the activity and the learning experience.
• Identify the key learning points from the exercise.
• Label and reinforce the learning points, as you would do for a case study. |

Assembling the Instructor's Guide

After preparing the instructor's notes and instructions for administering the learning activities, you assemble them into an instructor's guide. Usually you do so through your word processor or desktop publishing program. A typical instructor's guide follows this structure:

1. title page (same as for student guide, but with the words "Instructor's Guide" on the cover)
2. table of contents (most word processors will automatically produce this; see the next chapter for information on how)
3. edition notice (page with copyright statements)
4. setup instructions
5. visuals with instructor's notes on the page
6. learning activities, including both the student version and the instructor's version (including guide to leading the debriefing instruction)
7. close-out list.

The Basics of Preparing Workbook-Based Courses

The materials for a workbook-based course include the lecture, which usually takes the form of annotated slides similar to the ones you would include in an instructor's guide for a classroom course but written in complete sentences or a book-like narrative; exercises and learning activities; solutions to these exercises and learning activities (much as you would find in an instructor's guide for a classroom course, but written to be read by learners); and supplemental information.

Preparing a workbook-based course is, in many ways, like preparing a classroom course, with a few adjustments. Table 7-4 suggests the structure of a workbook course, and how preparing these materials differs from preparing them for a classroom course.

Basic Rule 23
Include all the material needed to complete the course in a workbook because learners have no other source of instruction or guidance.

Table 7-4. Structure of a workbook-based course.

Item	How to Prepare
Title Page	Same as you would do for a classroom course
Table of Contents	Same as you would do for a classroom course
Edition Notice	Same as you would do for a classroom course; also include a list of trademarks used in the workbook (if any)
Visuals or Other Means of Presentation	Different organizations take a different approach to presenting this material. • Some present visuals with notes. Unlike the instructor's notes, which really are notes, the notes accompanying visuals in a student book are complete thoughts, written in complete sentences. • Some write the material as if they were writing a manual. (Note that learners do not have direct access to an instructor when reading the learning material, so make sure that it is clear enough for nearly all learners to understand on the first reading, without assistance.)
Exercises	Because learners do not have direct access to instructors while taking a workbook-based course, the instructions are as detailed as those provided to an instructor in a classroom course. The workbook also contains the following: • Solution to the exercise • Hints, which help learners past known trouble spots • Notes about the exercise, which are a summary of the comments that would have been presented in a debriefing in a classroom course.
Supplemental Information	Same as you would do for a classroom course
References and Other Resources	Same as you would do for a classroom course
Evaluation Form	Provide instructions on how to submit the evaluation. If the learner must mail the evaluation, provide an addressed, postage-paid envelope to simplify this process.

Getting It Done

The materials that you prepare for a course vary depending on whether the course is classroom or workbook-based. For a classroom course, you prepare a student guide, which contains visuals, instructions for performing the exercises, and supplemental information. You also prepare an instructor's guide, which contains annotated visuals from which instructors lecture, and annotated instructions for administering exercises.

A workbook-based course contains material that is similar to that prepared for the classroom but is prepared so that the learner can use it without the involvement of an instructor.

Regardless of the medium of instruction, all learning materials and activities should directly relate to the learning objectives of the course. Materials and activities that do not relate to the objectives distract learners and make mastering the objectives that much more difficult.

Use exercise 7-1 to guide you through the decisions made in developing the materials for the course. It provides a checklist of issues you might address.

Exercise 7-1. Preparing materials for your course.

Preparing Materials for Classroom Courses	
Preparing the Student Guide	Preparing the visuals • Begin with a title? ☐ Yes ☐ No • Keep the total number of words to 35 or fewer? ☐ Yes ☐ No • Provide a record, not a transcript, of the content? ☐ Yes ☐ No Preparing exercises and supplemental information • Begin with a heading that explains the purpose of the activity? ☐ Yes ☐ No • Provide instructions for completing the activity? ☐ Yes ☐ No • Provide hints for handling known trouble spots? ☐ Yes ☐ No • Provide forms for recording information (if needed)? ☐ Yes ☐ No Assembling the student guide • Include the following at the beginning of the guide: title page, edition notice, and table of contents? ☐ Yes ☐ No • Include the following at the end of the guide: list of references and evaluation form? ☐ Yes ☐ No
Preparing the Instructor's Guide	Preparing the setup instructions: Did you include the following (when appropriate): Audiovisual requirements, other equipment and software needed, room setup, and information about preparing for hands-on exercises? ☐ Yes ☐ No

(continued on page 136)

135

Exercise 7-1. Preparing materials for your course (continued).

| Preparing the Instructor's Guide (continued) | Preparing the annotated visuals: Do they include notes rather than a word-for-word script?
☐ Yes ☐ No

Preparing instructions for administering learning activities: Did you include:
• introductory material?
☐ Yes ☐ No

• annotated instructions, which include instructions for helping learners with known trouble spots?
☐ Yes ☐ No

• description of the solution?
☐ Yes ☐ No

• guide to leading the post-activity debriefing?
☐ Yes ☐ No

Assembling the instructor's guide:
• Include the following at the beginning of the guide: title page, edition notice, and table of contents?
☐ Yes ☐ No

• Include the following at the end of the guide: list of references and the evaluation form?
☐ Yes ☐ No |

Preparing Materials for Workbook-based Course

| Preparing the Workbook | Did you include the following:
• Title page?
☐ Yes ☐ No

• Table of contents?
☐ Yes ☐ No

• Edition notice (page with copyright statements)?
☐ Yes ☐ No

• Visuals with a complete narrative accompanying them or other means of presenting the learning content?
☐ Yes ☐ No |

Exercise 7-1. Preparing materials for your course (continued).

Preparing the Workbook (continued)	• Exercises, which include not only the exercise, but also hints for addressing known problem spots and solutions? ☐ Yes ☐ No • Supplemental information? ☐ Yes ☐ No • List of references and other sources of information? ☐ Yes ☐ No • Evaluation form? ☐ Yes ☐ No

This chapter identified the specific materials you need to develop when developing classroom and workbook-based courses. Chapter 8 offers specific suggestions for writing, designing, and producing these materials with your word processor or desktop publishing program.

8

The Basics of Producing
Learning Materials

What's Inside This Chapter

This chapter explains how to produce the materials used in classroom and workbook-based courses. Specifically this chapter explains the following:

▶ Basic techniques for communicating learning content
▶ Basics of producing visuals
▶ Basics of producing workbooks
▶ Basics of the production process.

In addition, a worksheet at the end of this chapter guides you through the process of producing these course materials.

Getting Started

Production is the process that transforms the completed draft of the training materials into a form that can be used by learners. For example, production is the process that turns a draft of slides and a bunch of exercises into bound student's and instructor's guides.

39

In many organizations, course designers and developers are responsible for producing the final copy of their courses. This chapter explains that process. The majority of it explains how to finalize the messages and designs for your visuals and workbooks (whether those workbooks support a classroom course or if they stand alone). Then, it explains the steps in preparing materials for use by learners and instructors.

Techniques for Communicating Learning Content

Learners do not know the content of your training program, so if the explanations are not clear, learners won't be able to master the objectives after finishing the course. Similarly, many learners have limited confidence in their ability to master the objectives. The words that you choose and messages that you convey can help build this confidence and minimize frustration.

Following are some suggestions for presenting learning content as clearly and supportively as possible.

Basic Rule 24
Always communicate clearly and supportively.

Ensure That Content Relates to Learning Objectives

Yes, this point has been mentioned before. But, as you move further into the development process, material that does not relate to the objectives more easily slips into the course materials. For example, a SME might ask you to include something and you do so as a favor, or you might find something interesting that you want to share with learners. Despite the good intentions for including this material, it only distracts learners from the objectives and makes achieving those objectives all the more difficult.

Use Analogies, Examples, and Stories

As discussed in chapter 1, adult learners learn best when they can relate to the material on some level. One way to relate the material is by using analogies, examples, and stories. Consider these examples:

- To explain how a simple conversation can cause a security breach, a course designer and developer might include stories about conversations that had been overheard and resulted in leaks about upcoming products in the trade press.
- To explain the concept of two-tiered security involving user IDs and passwords in the security course, a course designer and developer might compare them to deadbolt locks or security alarm systems used in many homes. This comparison is called an *analogy*.
- To prepare learners for conducting their first employee appraisal, an instructor in an introductory course on supervision might relate the experience of the first appraisal she gave.

Using examples, analogies, and stories offers many benefits. In some instances, they make abstract concepts more concrete. In the first situation, many people might think that an innocent conversation among co-workers is just that, not realizing that reporters might purposely eavesdrop and report what they hear.

Analogies play a similar role. They present a new concept (user IDs and passwords) in terms of a familiar one (locks and security alarms on homes).

Stories work in some ways like examples, but they also add human emotions to the presentation. By relating how she felt about conducting her first employee appraisal, the instructor in the third example could address directly some of the emotions that learners might have when conducting theirs.

In addition to making abstract points seem more concrete, you can use examples, analogies, and stories to reinforce learning by referring back to them and building on them throughout a training program. Seeing the examples, analogies, and stories in different units reinforces points for learners and allows them to easily see relationships among content categories. Similarly, course designers and developers reinforce and deepen learning by building on the same explanations, examples, and graphics in different units. For example, notice how designs for courses on security procedures and supervision keep appearing in this book.

Reinforce Learning Through Repetition

Using the same phrases and terms throughout the course builds familiarity with new concepts. For example, when introducing a concept at the beginning of a unit, referring to it during the unit, and summarizing it at the end of the unit, use the same phrases. By using the same phrases, learners realize that you are trying to make the same point. As with examples, this purposeful repetition reinforces learning.

Use Images to Communicate

In fact, you can communicate certain messages more effectively through visuals than with words. In many instances, a picture is easier to understand than text, and frequently learners remember pictures better than words. Whenever possible and appropriate, use images rather than text.

Communicating visually presents a challenge to most course designers and developers, who are primarily trained to use words to communicate. As a result, many course designers and developers believe they must be able to draw to effectively use visuals. Not true. Rather, they need to be able to choose the right type of image. A professional illustrator or graphic designer can assist with preparation of the actual image. In other words, you might not actually create the graphic image yourself, but it results from your thinking of it.

Specifically when might a visual be helpful? Table 8-1 provides some suggestions.

Use a Positive, Supportive Tone

As you develop learning content, you not only present content needed to achieve the learning objectives, but you also motivate learners to believe they can master them. One way of doing so is emphasizing the positive and using a supportive tone.

Table 8-1. Choosing images for your course.

When You Need to Show:	Use This Type of Image:
Financial Figures	If you are showing relationships of parts to a whole (like the division of a budget), use a pie chart. If you are showing financial figures over time, use bar charts.
Trends Over Time	Use bar charts, also called histograms (which use a single point to represent the financial figures for each point in time).
Products	For pre-sales efforts such as marketing, use a photograph. For post-sales efforts (like troubleshooting), use a line drawing. A line drawing is easier to follow for the purposes of technical training because it only shows the most relevant details. Photographs show extraneous details, and these details often distract learners.
A Sequence	Use a flow chart, which shows how one point flows to the next.
Relationships	Use an organizational chart or a map.

Although learners ultimately make their own assessment of the overall tone, certain communication tips can help you build a more supportive tone. These include

- *emphasizing the positive.* When presenting content, avoid words like *don't* and *not;* they emphasize things that learners can't do. Instead, emphasize what learners can do. When advising against something, use the word *avoid.*

- *avoiding presumptions.* In attempts to lower the anxiety levels of learners, course designers and developers often use expressions like, "It'll be easy" and "That's simple." Indeed, these may be the goals. But, imagine these phrases from the learner's perspective. Suppose a learner hears material that the course designer calls "easy," but that the learner has difficulty mastering. Labeling the material as "easy" only makes the learner feel worse, because he or she can't even master easy content. Avoiding words like "easy" and "simple" helps you avoid presuming how learners might feel about the content.

Also avoid terms that presume other ways that learners might feel about the material, such as "Don't you like this?" or "It will make your work easier." This is tempting when introducing a change that learners are expected to resist. But using such expressions does not change learners' points of views. Indeed, these expressions often reinforce old points of view.

Avoid Technical Jargon

After immersing yourself in the content as you analyzed the needs, developed the objectives, and planned the presentation of the content, and working closely with SMEs, you might learn to speak about the content in a shorthand of sorts. This shorthand is called *technical jargon.*

Most learners will not know this jargon, because they have not yet learned the subject. Rather than ask the instructor to define unfamiliar terms, many learners will sit and do nothing, for fear of looking stupid. But if learners don't understand the

Noted

Some SMEs suggest that you'll insult learners by avoiding technical terms. Ignore this well-intentioned advice. Most learners will not speak up if they do not know a term. If you feel that many learners already know what a term means, you can handle the situation by beginning the definition with comments like "As many of you are already aware" or "To make sure that we're working with similar definitions. . . ."

terms used in the training program, they cannot understand the technical content. And, if learners cannot understand the technical content, they cannot master the objectives.

So avoid unnecessary technical terms whenever possible. When you cannot, define technical terms the first time that you use them in a training program. If you do not use a term again until another unit, define it again. Learners might have forgotten it. Also, provide a glossary with the student materials so learners can review definitions.

Basic Rules for Preparing Visuals

This section explains how to design visible, legible, and clear visuals for a classroom course—both slides and transparencies. *Visible* means that learners can see the letters and images on the slide in the back row of the classroom in which the visuals are used. *Legible* means that the images on the slide are easily deciphered by learners. *Clear* means that learners can decipher the message on the first read-through. Unless stated otherwise, the guidelines apply to both types of visuals.

Become Familiar with the Basic Grid of the Visual

As mentioned in the last chapter and shown in figure 7-1, a slide is typically divided into two key areas. Although the heading area always contains a heading, the content area can contain the following:

- ▸ text only (most likely, bullet points)
- ▸ graphics only
- ▸ graphics with text labels
- ▸ text (such as bullet points) on one side, graphics on another
- ▸ table or chart.

Limit the Amount of Text on a Slide

As mentioned in the last chapter, the text on a slide is intended to serve as a reminder of key points, not a transcript of the lecture. On any one slide:

- ▸ limit the total number of words to 35 (including the heading).
- ▸ limit the number of bullet points to five.
- ▸ limit the number of words for each bullet point to seven.

Basic Rule 25

Design slides to be visible and legible from the farthest corner of the classroom and clear at the first read-through.

When Using Bulleted or Numbered Lists, Make Sure That You Have at Least Two Items

Often the best way to emphasize your key points is through the use of bulleted or numbered lists. Just make sure that you have at least two items. Otherwise, use a paragraph format. A single bullet point looks odd, as though something's missing.

When Presenting Bullet Points, Use Parallel Grammatical Construction

A parallel grammatical construction is one in which each bullet point begins with the same type of word (verb or noun). When one bullet point follows a different structure, it calls attention to itself but distracts learners from the message at hand. They focus, instead, on the question, "Why does this bullet point look weird?" For example, consider the third bullet item in figure 8-1. It looks like it does not belong on the list.

Figure 8-1. Failure to use parallel construction makes for an awkwardly worded slide.

Goals for the Coming Year

- Grow 10.3 percent next year
- Increase sales
- Costs
- Acquire new companies

Use Capitalization Judiciously

Avoid the tendency to overuse capitalization in your text. Generally, you can use these guidelines for capitalization:

► For headings, capitalize the first letter of each word except articles (such words as *a, an,* and *the*) and prepositions (such words as *of, by,* and *to*).

► Capitalize the first letter of the first word of each bullet point. Do not capitalize other words except for proper names. Proper names include the full names of organizations, the names of countries and people, and the proper names of departments and products. Do not capitalize generic department names, such as sales and engineering or the generic names of products, such as computers and pharmaceuticals.

Consider the example in figure 8-2, in which terms are properly capitalized. Notice that engineering and sales are not capitalized, because neither is a proper name.

Use Type Properly and Effectively

Any discussion of typography must begin with definitions of some common terms because conversations about this subject extensively use terminology:

► Serif or sans? According to Brusaw, Alred, and Oliu (2000), "Typography is characterized by the presence or absence of serifs. . . . A serif is a 'small projection

Figure 8-2. Proper capitalization on a slide.

New Positions

- Hanson is appointed Vice President.
- Mikush moves to the engineering unit.
- Fortis takes over the sales unit.

at end of a stroke of a letter.'" *Serif* type contains serifs; *sans serif* type does not. (Note that the word *sans* means without.) For an example, see table 8-2.

> ▶ A *typeface* is a particular look or design for the set of characters, and a *type font* is a complete set of characters in one typeface.

Limit the Number of Type Fonts on a Slide. Use at most two fonts—one for the headings, the other for body type (bullet points). (Of course, you can use just one font for both headings and body type.)

Use a Legible Type Size. Another consideration is the size of the type. Type is measured in a unit called a *point*. One point is 1/72 of an inch. Most type for reading is between 8 and 14 point. However, for slides there are different recommended guidelines:

> ▶ For headings, use 40- to 48-point type.
> ▶ For bullets, use 32- to 40-point type.
> ▶ For captions and callouts, use 24- to 32-point type.

Figure 8-3 shows some examples of different type sizes on a slide.

Appropriately Use Emphasis Type. Although emphasis type such as bold and italic is supposed to call attention to text, publishing convention limits the use of each to particular instances. Furthermore, the excessive use of emphasis type works counter to the original intentions: rather than calling attention to text, it draws attention away from it. For these reasons, use emphasis type as suggested in table 8-3.

Table 8-2. Some basic serif and sans serif typefaces.

Serif	Sans Serif
Century Schoolbook	Arial
Georgia	Helvetica
Palatino Linotype	Tekton
Times New Roman	Verdana
Bodoni	Stone Sans

Figure 8-3. Example of type size in a slide.

Point Size

- Points are a printer's measurement system
  — 1 point = 1/72 of an inch
  — 6 points = 1 pica
- Examples

word   word   word   word

20   28   36   44

Table 8-3. When to use special type attributes.

Bold	Bold type is used for headings, broadly defined here to include headings on charts and tables. It may also be used for captions.
Italic	Italicized text denotes titles of published works (books, videos, CDs, software) (such as *The Grapes of Wrath*). Italics are also used for words that are appropriated from other languages and have not become standard English (such as *détente*)
Underscore	Do not use underscoring, which has come to signify hyperlinks in text.
Color	For slides, use light colors for type (a cream for headings and a slightly lighter shade of cream for body text). In printed text and overhead transparencies, use black type. Avoid blue for type because blue is used in conjunction with underscoring to indicate hyperlinks.
ALL CAPS	Avoid using all caps except for acronyms and abbreviations. This approach to emphasizing text fails on two levels. On a physical level, learners have more difficulty reading text that is all uppercase than they do with mixed-case letters because learners have a difficult time distinguishing among the capital letters. On an emotional level, learners usually perceive all capitalized type as being yelled at.

Use Contrast to Distinguish Text and Background

A high contrast is one in which learners can easily distinguish the letters and images on the slide. The sharper the contrast between letters and images, and the background, the easier learners can read them. Create a high contrast between text and the background of the visual by applying the guidelines in table 8-4.

Table 8-4. Use the right background for your slides and transparencies.

Type of Image	Text	Background
Slides	Light (ideally white or cream-colored)	Slides use a dark background (ideally dark blue, charcoal gray, or dark brown) because they are intended to be used in a partially lit room.
Transparencies	Dark (ideally black) (creates the best contrast with a light background)	Transparencies use a light background (ideally clear, which will project as white) because they are intended to be used in a fully lit room.

Judiciously Use Animation on Slides

Animation is a sequence of graphics on a single slide that appears to learners as if the images move. You can only use animation with visuals directly projected from a computer.

Some of the most common animation techniques include

Noted

- ▶ displaying text one line at a time on a slide to help focus class discussion on one point at a time
- ▶ showing movement in a process
- ▶ making transitions among slides.

Prepare Visuals for Use as Handouts

Participants expect a copy of the visuals for handouts. Programs such as Microsoft PowerPoint let you easily create copies for handouts. Before printing, make sure that

Watch out for overuse of animation; it can quickly become distracting or annoying. Annoying uses of animation include noisy animation, like swoosh sounds used in transitions, typing sounds used when displaying lines one at a time, and the overuse of displaying text one line at a time. (If you use it on every slide, it loses its power to focus discussions.)

you include slide numbers on each slide. Also, think about whether you should distribute the handouts before or after the presentation.

Noted

To add slide numbers in PowerPoint, choose View from the Menu bar, then choose the Header and Footer option. Check the box beside Slide Number to include slide numbers. Learners like to have slide numbers in printouts so they can easily refer back to a slide. When printing, choose the Handouts option under Print What.

Typically, course designers prepare the handouts in one of these ways:

▶ *three slides per page:* When using PowerPoint, lines for taking notes are usually prepared beside the slide.

▶ *two slides per page:* The images are larger, so learners have an easier time reading the text after class.

The Basics of Preparing Workbooks

This section explains how to design the pages for workbooks—both the materials that supplement a classroom course and workbooks that stand alone as courses. The suggestions that follow help you design pages that are easy to read. Unless stated otherwise, the guidelines apply to both types of workbooks.

Become Familiar with the Basic Grid of the Page

As mentioned earlier in this chapter, the slide is typically divided into two key areas. Pages, too, have a basic grid, as shown in figure 8-4.

Leave 25 Percent of the Page as White Space

White space includes the margins as well as space between paragraphs and text and images. White space provides a rest from long blocks of text; visually separates items,

Basic Rule 26

Design pages for easy reading. As you design pages for a workbook—whether they're student materials for a classroom course or a workbook that stands alone as a course—the choices that you make can either make reading an easier or more difficult experience.

Figure 8-4. General grid of a page.

	Margin (room for running header)	
Margin	HEADING Content Area	Margin
	Margin (room for running footer and slide number)	

such as pictures from text, one paragraph from another, and headings from the passages that follow; and serves as margins, which provide a border of sorts for the page.

Studies suggest that you should leave 25 percent of the page as white space. When checking your page designs, make sure that you:

- ▶ leave a margin at the top and bottom of the page
- ▶ leave a margin around the central block of content on the page
- ▶ leave space between blocks of content, such as between a block of text and an illustration
- ▶ indent the first line of a paragraph or leave a blank line between paragraphs
- ▶ leave some space between a heading and the text that follows.

Also use your eye to determine whether white space is needed. If a page looks a little full with text, add white space to the area that looks crowded.

Limit the Number of Typefaces on a Page

As suggested for designing visuals, use at most two typefaces on a page—one for the headings, the other for body text.

Furthermore, make sure that the two typefaces coordinate nicely; the typeface that you choose for headings should look good with the typeface you choose for body text. Generally, if you choose a serif font for one, choose a sans serif font for the other. For example, if you choose a sans serif font like Helvetica for headings, you might choose a serif font like Bodoni for the body text (see table 8-2).

Design Pages for "Scanability"

One of the challenges learners face when using workbooks is locating information. By using typography effectively and including devices such as page numbers and running headers, you can help readers find the content they seek.

Use Headings

Headings are especially important in workbooks because they help learners easily find content on a page. A typical learner scans the headings to identify the importance of the various sections and identify the content covered in it. The size of the heading in relation to other headings signifies the importance of the section that follows: the larger the type size, the more significant the section.

By using a consistent system of headings, course designers and developers can signal information to learners. The system is characterized by levels of headings. The lower the heading number, the larger its size and the more significant the material that follows. Table 8-5 shows a typical scheme for formatting headings.

Table 8-5. Some examples of typefaces for headings.

Heading Level	Type Size
Heading 1	16-point bold
Heading 2	14-point bold
Heading 3	The same as the type of body text (regular text), either 11 or 12 point bold
Heading 4	The same as the type of body text (regular text), either 11 or 12 point bold and italic.

Specific guidelines for preparing headings include using only one typeface for all the headings and distinguishing differences among headings with type size.

Use Appropriate-Sized Body Type

Body type is the text of the workbook. Generally, 12-point text makes reading easiest, especially if you have a number of learners over age 40 when many people become near-sighted.

If you have a limited amount of space, you may lower the size of the type to 11 or 10 point. But be aware that, at 10 point, some learners will have difficulty reading the type.

Also, remember to use emphasis type appropriately, following the same guidelines recommended for visuals.

Noted

Most word processing and desktop publishing systems are designed so that you can enter headings according to their level. The way that you indicate whether or not text is a heading (and, if it is a heading, its level) is through the use of named styles. Named styles are instructions to an authoring system. Each named style has formatting information associated with it; that information is stored in another file. Every time the system encounters text in that named style, it uses the instructions for formatting it from the other file.

If you want to change the appearance of headings or text, you would change the formatting instructions stored in the other file; you do not need to change every instance of that type of heading (which could become cumbersome if you have hundreds of headings). In addition, some text processors can "read" named styles and use them to automatically generate a table of contents.

Finally, if you choose to change authoring systems, many will keep the named styles so you do not need to reformat the text when you transfer it.

Appropriately Justify Text

Justification refers to the alignment of text on the margin. *Left justification* refers to aligning text along the left margin. Most text is left justified. *Right justification* refers to aligning text on the right margin. *Centering* text places text equally distant from either margin. You can also justify text on both the left and right margins (full justification). Margins that are not justified are called *ragged.*

Noted

Do not use full justification. To make sure that the text justifies on both margins, the computer must either stretch the letters or add many extra spaces. Either way, the type looks strange and interferes with reading. This guideline also pertains to designing visuals.

Despite all of these choices, it is recommended that you only justify text on the left margin.

Plan a Clean, Simple Layout

Layout refers to the arrangement of elements on the page. Thoughtful arrangement of them can simplify the task of learning, help learners distinguish the most important content, draw attention to content that learners might overlook and, perhaps most significantly, attract and maintain attention. Of course, incompletely thought-out layouts can have the opposite effect.

Keep these guidelines in mind as you plan your layout:

- ▷ Place the most important content at the upper right corner of a right-hand page. This is the first place that learners look for content when opening a two-page spread of a workbook. For this reason, you might notice that most workbooks start new sections on a right-hand page.
- ▷ Design standard layouts for recurring types of pages. Although the content on each page in a workbook is unique, the type of content is not. Some pages present content as text, with graphics illustrating the key points. Some pages instruct learners to answer questions and later provide feedback on the responses. Some pages introduce a unit, others summarize it. (Notice how templates are used in this book for the opening and closing sections of each chapter, the sections Basic Rules, Think About This, and Noted.)

Help Learners Navigate the Workbook

Use running headers or footers on each page to indicate the page number, the name of the course, and the number and name of the unit. A running header is a header in small type that appears at the top of the page. A running footer is the same thing, but appears at the bottom of each page.

As mentioned elsewhere, a table of contents also helps learners easily find material in a workbook.

The Basics of the Production Process

Production—the process of preparing course materials for duplication—and related printing are relatively simple processes but involve numerous details. Missing a detail can cause significant problems, including delays in completing development of the training program.

The actual process of production involves converting the drafts of the various elements you have developed into pieces that can be combined into a master copy, then duplicating it. Specifically, production involves (1) copyediting text; (2) producing graphics; (3) combining the text and graphics into a single file; (4) making a backup copy of the master, and storing it in a safe place; (5) sending the master copy to print; and (6) assembling a complete course package.

Basic Rule 27
Production and printing are about attending to details.

Copyediting Text

Copyediting, a topic covered in chapter 9, is the process of marking text for final typesetting. Copyediting begins after your sponsor has approved all of the text and released it for publication. The copyeditor looks for errors with grammar and style, raises possible legal issues, and makes sure that the production staff has adequate instructions for producing a communication product.

Producing Graphics

This part of the production process involves the conversion of ideas to concrete images. In some instances, you've already prepared the graphics as part of the process of developing earlier drafts. This might have happened if you are using clip art and other types of previously created images or if you have skills in creating graphics. But, if you are using photographs or hiring a graphic artist to prepare your graphics, you will most likely wait until the sponsor approves the final version of the training program before hiring an artist. If you hire someone earlier in the process and the information changes, you might have wasted the sponsor's funds.

Although the exact activities that you need to perform depend on the type of graphic images used in your training program, in general, producing graphics involves these activities:

- ▶ preparing original drawings, such as line drawings and icons
- ▶ preparing computer images, such as three-dimensional drawings
- ▶ taking photographs
- ▶ adding graphic touches to text, such as adding lines above and below headings.

Most likely, an illustrator will produce line drawings or icons. The illustrator might do this work by hand or on a computer but, ultimately, you want the image to be stored as a computer file so you can integrate it with the text and have it available for future use.

Another aspect of producing graphics is adapting drawings from other sources. When you adapt a drawing, you can

- ▶ add or remove features (such as adding color)
- ▶ change the size of an image
- ▶ crop the image, which involves cutting off part of the image and changing the image size.

In some cases, you can hire a graphic artist to take a basic image and add or remove features from it. In other cases, you might scan a picture into the computer from another source, such as a from a book or photograph and, using special graphics software like Adobe Photoshop, add and remove features and crop it. Or, you might use a combination of these.

When using photographs, note that, although you can find seemingly foolproof point-and-shoot cameras, hire a photographer to take the photographs for you. Point-and-shoot photography is primarily intended for personal use and does not work well for educational purposes. Industrial photography does, but requires extensive attention to lighting, placement of images, and other details.

Furthermore, if you intend to include people in your photographs, you need to consider such issues as hiring and preparing models and using model release forms (providing you with legal permission to use their images in your training program). A professional photographer can assist you with these issues, too.

After taking the photograph, the photographer, a graphic artist, or you can retouch it using special software or other tools. When you retouch a photograph, you can remove unnecessary details, such as an arm that is not attached to any person in the photograph, change the image size, remove blemishes, and enhance colors.

Combining Text and Graphics Into a Single File

Accomplishing this task involves the following activities:

▶ If you have not already done so, incorporate the suggestions of the copyeditor.

▶ Add the title page, copyright notice, evaluation forms, front and back covers, and other elements to the master copy of the course materials.

▶ Integrate graphics into the master file at the exact location where you would like to place them in the text.

▶ Check and correct any pagination problems. For example, if you start each chapter with the page number X-1 (where X is the number of the chapter), then make sure the first page of chapter 1 is 1-1 and the first page of chapter 2 is 2-1, etc.

▶ Generate the table of contents. Make sure that your word-processing program or desktop publisher has included every page and that it assigned the correct page numbers in the table of contents. This is one of the most important, although tedious, tasks. Specifically, make sure that every page is included in the master copy and that each has the proper page number and running header or footer. Check the master file to ensure that the table of contents is included and that the page numbers are correct. You especially need to perform this double-check if your desktop publishing program is automatically generating tables of contents, running headers or footers, and indexes.

You have now prepared the final copy. Get a clean copy of the printout.

Making a Backup of the Master Copy

Store the master in a safe place. In this backup copy, include both the source file and a printout. If anything should happen to the master copy, you have a duplicate.

Sending the Master Copy to the Printer

Your printer might require that you provide additional information and mark-up. If so, your printer's representative will explain what you need to do.

Assembling a Complete Course Package

After receiving the printed copies from the printer, assemble a package that includes a copy of the visuals (on CD or DVD if the instructor uses slides, printed on transparencies if the instructor uses an overhead projector), student materials (including the student guide you produced and other materials that might be distributed to learners), and instructor's guide.

Give this package to the administrators who will support the course and the instructors who will teach it.

Getting It Done

When producing materials for a classroom course, first finalize the messages. For communicating the content, make sure to communicate it clearly and supportively. Also, replace text with visuals whenever possible.

When designing slides, make sure that they are visible and legible from the farthest location of the room and that learners can understand them on the first read-through. When designing pages, design them for easy reading.

After preparing this material, produce it. Production involves myriad details; make sure that you tend to each.

Use exercise 8-1 to guide you through the decisions involved in communicating content and preparing for production. It provides a checklist of issues you might address and activities you need to consider.

Exercise 8-1. A checklist for producing learning materials.

Communicate Learning Content	☐ Use analogies, examples, and stories to make your points
	☐ Reinforce learning by using the same phrases and terms throughout the course
	☐ Use a positive and supportive tone
	___ Emphasize the positive
	___ Avoid presumptions in text
	☐ Avoid technical jargon
	___ Use plain language when possible
	___ Define terms the first time that you use them when you cannot use an equivalent term in plain language
Prepare Visuals	☐ Become familiar with the basic grid of the visual
	☐ Limit the
	___ Total number of words on the visual to 35
	___ Number of bullet points to five
	___ Number of words for each bullet point to seven
	☐ When using bulleted or numbered lists, make sure that you have at least two items
	☐ When presenting bullet points, use a parallel grammatical construction
	☐ Use capitalization sparingly
	☐ Limit the number of type fonts on a slide to two
	☐ Use appropriate-sized type
	___ For headings, use 40- to 48-point type
	___ For bullets, use 32- to 40-point type
	___ For captions and callouts, use 24- to 32-point type
	☐ Use emphasis type appropriately
	___ Bold—headings
	___ Italic—titles of published works or terms
	___ No underscoring
	___ No color for type
	___ Avoid all caps
	☐ Create a high contrast between text and the background of the visual
	___ Slides: light text on a dark background
	___ Transparencies: dark text on a light background
	☐ Carefully use animation on slides
	☐ Prepare visuals for use as handouts

(continued on page 160)

Exercise 8-1. A checklist for producing learning materials (continued).

Prepare Pages	
	☐ Become familiar with the basic grid of the page
	☐ Leave 25 percent of the page as white space
	☐ Limit the number of type fonts on a page to two—one for headings, the other for body text
	☐ Use appropriate type for headings
	___ Heading 1 (unit or chapter) 16 point
	___ Heading 2 (section) 14 point
	___ Heading 3 (sub-section) 11 or 12 point
	___ Heading 4 (sub-sub section) 11 or 12 point
	☐ Use appropriate-sized body type (ideally 12 point, but no smaller than 10 point)
	☐ Justify text on the left
	☐ Plan a clean, simple layout
	___ Place the most important content at the upper right corner of a right-hand page
	___ Design standard layouts for recurring types of pages
	☐ Help learners navigate through the workbook
Produce Components for Duplication	
	☐ Copyedit text
	☐ Produce graphics
	☐ Combine the text and graphics into a single file, and produce and prepare it for printing
	☐ Make a backup copy of the master, and store it in a safe place
	☐ Send the master copy to print
	☐ After receiving the printed copies from the printer, assemble a complete course package
	☐ Send the course package to the administrators who will support the course and the instructors who will teach it

This chapter explained how to prepare instructional materials. Chapter 9 explains how to make sure that materials are effective before you make them widely available.

The Basic Quality Checks for a New Course

What's Inside This Chapter

This chapter introduces you to the basics of reviewing a draft training program for effectiveness and making revisions to improve the likelihood of success when the training program becomes generally available. Specifically this chapter addresses the following:

▶ A discussion of formative evaluation, the process of evaluating a training program under development

▶ The three basic types of formative evaluation (pilot tests, technical reviews, and editorial and production reviews)

▶ The basics of revisions, including how to respond to feedback and revise materials.

In addition, a worksheet at the end of this chapter helps you plan for formative evaluation.

Basic Rule 28

Testing a training program with its intended learners is the only way to predict the likelihood of its success.

What Is Formative Evaluation?

One of the key challenges of preparing a training program is making sure that it will really accomplish the objectives for which you developed it. Assessing the effectiveness of a training program while it is under development is called *formative evaluation* because you assess it while it is being *form*ed. Formative evaluation contrasts with *summative evaluation,* which assesses the effectiveness of a training program that is generally available, such as a classroom course that is listed in a course catalog and available for enrollment, or a workbook that learners can order and use now. Kirkpatrick's four levels of evaluation, first introduced in chapter 1 and further discussed in chapter 4, provide a framework for approaching summative evaluation.

The sole purpose of a formative evaluation is improving the draft training program and increasing the likelihood that it will achieve its objectives when you make it generally available. As a result, you conduct a formative evaluation while the training program is under development and rather than report the results externally, you use this information to revise the training program now and make it more effective upon general availability.

Specifically, during formative evaluation, you try to make sure that the training program has these qualities:

▶ *understandable:* Learners should be able to comprehend content on the first explanation and follow exercises with no additional assistance, other than that provided in the instructions. Learners should not be slowed by inconsistencies in content, terminology, grammatical errors, or awkwardly presented content.

▶ *accurate:* The material should be current and correct.

▶ *functional:* Printed pages should match those on the screen in word processors. Slides should appear on the projector as they do on the computer screen. Addresses of Websites shown to the class should be accurate and working. Hands-on exercises should work as intended.

The Three Basic Types of Formative Evaluation

To make sure your course is understandable, accurate, and functional, you conduct three types of formative evaluations:

▶ pilot tests, in which you conduct the training program for the first time with people who represent the intended learners for the purpose of assessing which parts work and which ones need improvement

▶ technical reviews, in which SMEs verify the accuracy of the content

▶ production reviews, in which editors assess the completeness and style of the content, and production specialists make sure that the printed and projected output matches that which appears on the computer screen.

Pilot Tests

As mentioned earlier, a pilot test is one in which you take the training program for a trial run; that is, you run it for the first time to assess which parts work and which ones need improvement. You generally conduct a pilot test with the second draft of student materials and instructor's materials. Participants in the pilot class represent the intended learners. When you identify areas where the training program needs improvement, you try to pinpoint the specific improvements that you need to make.

Basic Rule 29

A pilot test tests the training program, not the learners.

The results of the pilot test are intended to assess whether or not the training program works. Because the training program has not been proven yet to be effective, you do not use the test results to assess the success of learners. You might find errors in the teaching sequence or in the wording of test questions, which limit the ability of learners to pass the course.

So, how do you go about conducting a pilot test? Following is a suggested procedure. You might need to adjust this procedure in your organization.

1. Well in advance of the class, reserve a room for the pilot class. Before doing so, make sure that the room has the audiovisual and computer equipment

needed (such as a data projector for PowerPoint slides and computers for every student for courses with computer-based labs), can be set up to meet your needs (for example, you might want learners to sit at tables so they can work in groups) and can accommodate the number of learners needed for the pilot class.

2. Recruit between eight and 15 learners to participate in the pilot class. If you recruit fewer, you might not receive a sufficiently broad perspective on the course. If you recruit more, you might not be able to debrief each learner and receive their comments. Learners should represent the demographics of the intended learners, and they should be supportive of the course.

3. If you are a course developer and someone else will be teaching the training program when it becomes generally available, also recruit an instructor to teach the pilot class so you can assess the effectiveness of the instructor's materials.

4. Between two and five working days before the class is scheduled, send a reminder to all of the participants.

5. Print and copy learners' materials, including copies of slides and drafts of the student materials.

6. At the beginning of the class session, remind learners that this is a pilot class and that it is a test of the training program, not them. In other words, if learners do not understand something or feel that instructions could be clarified, learners should assume that the problem is with the training materials. They should flag any problems and make relevant comments in their student materials. Let the learners know that after each unit, you will stop the class to request feedback from them.

7. Teach.

8. At appropriate intervals, stop the learning and ask for feedback. This is called a *debriefing*. Some instructors like to debrief a pilot class after every unit because the comments on it are still "fresh" with learners. Others like to debrief at the end of each day, to avoid interrupting the flow of the class. Choose an interval that feels comfortable to you. Begin the debriefing by reminding learners again that the pilot test is a test of the training program, not them. Second, ask the learners a series of questions: How do they feel about the material taught so far? Are there specific areas where information and instructions were unclear? What about the material works well? Do they have specific suggestions for change?

9. At the end of the class session, conduct a final debriefing that considers the entire training program, not just a single unit. At this debriefing, ask learners for overall impressions about the parts of the training program that were effective and the parts that could be changed.

Noted

To avoid the appearance of bias, you might ask a colleague to conduct the debriefing. Also, because a colleague is facilitating the discussion, you can record the comments on your copies of materials.

Encourage learners to provide specific suggestions on ways to fix the problems they identified—the more specific their feedback, the better you can address their concerns.

10. Assess learners' performance on tests and other assessments to make sure that questions really address the objectives, that learners understand the test questions, and that learners have been taught the material so they have an opportunity to answer correctly.

After completing the pilot test, review your notes. Categorize proposed comments as *A* (showstoppers—design and development should not continue before you address these issues), *B* (must change—although design and development can continue, you must address these issues before making the training program generally available), and *C* (nice to change—comments that you will address if your time permits). Using these comments and their priorities as a guide, revise the training program.

Noted

If you have recruited an instructor to teach the pilot class, also debrief the instructor. Find out which information the instructor felt was clear, and which information the instructor felt uncomfortable teaching. Also ask the instructor to identify places in the instructor's materials where content could be made more effective.

Technical Reviews

Typically, course designers and developers request technical reviews for each draft of the training program that they produce, except the final one. In a technical review,

SMEs verify the accuracy of the content. Technical reviews are especially important because incorrect technical information could pose a serious legal liability.

In regulated industries, such as the pharmaceutical industry, incorrect content could cause learners to perform their jobs incorrectly, and that could create a life-threatening situation (such as a doctor prescribing the wrong medicine). With new products that are not yet complete (this is especially true with software), the training program could provide incorrect instructions or refer to material that has significantly changed, causing frustration and other potential problems for learners. For content that has high visibility or sensitivity within an organization, such as management training, the content presented must represent a consensus of opinion among leaders. Otherwise, learners might follow policies and approaches on the job that key decision makers do not support or that are inconsistent within the organization. Two types of technical reviews exist: reading and walk-through.

Reading Reviews. During a reading review, designated people read through the draft of the training program and assess its effectiveness according to a certain set of criteria. The criteria vary, depending on the reviewer's perspective and expertise. For example, a SME might review a draft to assess whether the technical content is accurate. A marketing specialist might review a draft to assess whether the training program is going to reach the intended audience. And, a sponsor might review a draft to assess whether the intended users will be able to achieve the intended objectives with the training program.

Basic Rule 30

The best way to ensure that the content is technically accurate is by asking several SMEs to simultaneously review the training program.

To make sure that you receive the most helpful review comments, consider following this suggested procedure when conducting reading reviews:

1. At the beginning of the project, as soon as you set the schedule, notify reviewers about the dates of upcoming reviews, so they can plan ahead. When scheduling these reviews, make sure that you leave enough time for them.

Generally, leave at least one day of review for each 100 pages of review material. Also, if you send paper materials, leave at least two days at either end of the review to make copies and to provide time for people to mail responses back.

2. A few days before sending out each draft for review, send a reminder note that the review draft is coming.

3. Send the review draft. Accompany it with either an email message or a memo (depending on whether you send the draft electronically or by mail) in which you explain what reviewers should and should not do. You want them to comment on the accuracy of the content, the flow of the material, and ways to make the information clearer. You don't want them to focus on layout, which is likely to change, or grammatical issues, which are usually addressed later in the process.

4. After sending review drafts, send a reminder with the date that you expect to receive comments.

5. After receiving comments, go through each one and determine whether you intend to incorporate it. If you have questions (for example, if one comment contradicts a comment made by another reviewer), make notes, and then follow up with the reviewers or call a review meeting to discuss the questions. If you do not plan to incorporate a comment, briefly explain why. Finally, send an acknowledgment to each reviewer.

6. After you have incorporated the comments, send a follow-up note describing the status of the comments.

Walk-Throughs. In some instances, a reading review, in which reviewers read through the draft and write comments, does not elicit the extent of feedback that you need to ensure the accuracy of the training program. In such instances, you would consider conducting a series of walk-throughs.

In a walk-through, reviewers meet and use the meeting time to read through the printed drafts of the student and instructor's materials. The group walks through each page of the materials, and reviewers make their comments at that time. If a difference of opinion arises, the group resolves it then.

Walk-throughs are especially useful for:

▶ products and software for which the course designer and developer do not have access to prototypes

> ▸ abstract processes, such as troubleshooting, for which no single correct procedure exists

> ▸ instances in which SMEs have a history of conducting lax reviews, and the only way to get reviews from them is by locking them in a room.

When preparing for a walk-through, schedule a series of meetings—one for each unit of the training program—rather than a single meeting to address the entire program. Schedule two or three hours for each walk-through meeting. Also schedule the meetings on consecutive days for a period of one or two weeks, rather than stretching them out over an extended time.

Production Reviews

For a production review, editors assess the completeness and style of the content, and production specialists make sure that the printed and projected outputs (that is, slides projected from the computer or transparencies projected from an overhead projector) match that which appears on the computer screen.

Basic Rule 31
Although heavily focused on details, production reviews are essential to the success of the training program.

Many course designers and developers dismiss production reviews as services that add little value because they look at focused issues, like capitalization and type fonts. But, a small typographical error can cause a significant change in meaning, and layout problems can cause problems for learners. A significant number of grammatical errors can detract from the credibility of a training program, as some learners reason, "If they can't get their spelling straight, how can I be sure that they have the facts straight?" Taking production reviews seriously helps make sure that training programs maintain their credibility and accuracy.

Editors usually conduct production reviews. An editor serves as the "first learner" of a training program. As the first learner, the editor addresses a wide range of issues that, if not addressed, could cause problems. An example would be a glaring misspelling on a slide. In most organizations, editors only review a training program once—usually, just before it goes to final production.

At this point, editors typically focus on mechanics: grammar, usage, spelling, punctuation, and other mechanical aspects of text. This task of making sure that copy is grammatically and stylistically correct is called copyediting. Copyediting specifically looks at issues like these:

▶ editorial style, including usage, spelling, punctuation, capitalization, consistency of terminology, parallelism, and levels of headings

▶ layout of slides and pages to ensure consistency of design across student and instructor materials; appropriate use of templates (standard designs) for slides and pages; correct and consistent use of headings from slide to slide and page to page; consistent style for tables and charts; proper placement of illustrations and graphics; clearly marked and observed margins; correct usage of typefaces, especially emphasis type (such as bold and italic).

Editors also serve a more substantive role, working closely with course developers to fortify the structure of their courses, to identify and resolve unclear passages, and to enhance the presentation of information so that learners can easily understand it. This communication coaching is called *substantive editing* and is one of the key benefits that an editor brings to the course. But substantive editing must occur earlier in the development process, usually after the first draft.

The Basics of Revision

With the feedback that you receive through each type of review, you revise the draft of the training program. The following sections explore two issues that arise during revision: responding to feedback and revising the training program.

Think About This

Because many training organizations do not have editors on staff, course designers and developers perform editorial duties when reviewing one another's courses. This is called *peer editing* because peers (co-workers) perform the editing. If your organization does not provide access to editors, definitely seek a peer edit. You often cannot see some of the most glaring typographical and stylistic errors because you have such a close relationship to the course. A second set of eyes is helpful. Furthermore, if a peer is only available to review the training program once, schedule that review for the last draft, to ensure that the final product is free of mechanical, stylistic, and visual errors.

Responding to Feedback

One of the most challenging aspects of a course designer and developer's job is receiving comments on your work. Some comments might not make you feel good about your work. Other comments might not make you feel bad, but are so vague that they don't help you do a better job. Responding to such comments with dignity and grace is one of the true tests of professionalism for any course designer and developer.

Basic Rule 32

Assume all feedback has value, so make sure that you understand the comments and how the reviewer or editor is trying to improve the training program.

Consider the following suggestions for responding to feedback:

▶ Whenever possible, schedule comments to arrive on a Monday or Tuesday. By receiving comments on a Monday or Tuesday, you can immediately begin work on correcting them instead of brooding about them all weekend long.

▶ Wait one business day before formally responding to any comments. At the least, the extra day gives you an opportunity to calm down, should any comment raise your blood pressure. At the most, the extra time gives you chance to plot a course of action.

▶ Try to understand where reviews and edits are coming from. Sometimes, in the haste of reviewing, reviewers make comments without thinking about what they are saying and are unintentionally abrupt. In other cases, they write only part of what they are actually thinking, and you might be arriving at conclusions based on incomplete data.

▶ Speak to the reviewer or editor. Rather than avoid the situation, face it head on—and with an open mind.

▶ When responding to vague or derogatory comments, tell the reviewer or editor that you need some clarification on the comment. As best as possible, explain what you do not understand. By avoiding a value judgment ("That comment is useless!"), you can start a meaningful conversation.

These approaches open a dialogue without creating a confrontation and, in the process, forge a stronger relationship with the reviewer. Through dialogues like this, other course designers and developers have often found value in the comments, and reviewers better appreciate the work of course designers and developers.

Revising the Training Program

The way in which you manage a proposed change depends on its nature.

Noted

Admittedly, this section has primarily focused on negative feedback from reviewers. Those types of comments seem to command our attention. But, rest assured that reviewers often have positive comments to share, too, like "Great job," "Excellent work," and an old favorite, "This is the best user's guide we've ever seen!"

You can make two general categories of changes to a training program during the revision process: within scope and outside of scope.

Within-Scope Changes. These are changes that fall within the scope of the original assignment. To a large extent, within-scope changes represent a commitment to make a change and you should make them.

Within-scope changes include changes you committed to during the review process. As one of the last parts of the pilot test and technical and editorial reviews, you made commitments to reviewers to make certain revisions. When they see the next review draft, these people expect to see the changes incorporated.

When you incorporate these types of changes, you closely follow the essence of the suggested change. In some cases, this means incorporating the requested change verbatim. For example, if an attorney changes all of the instances of the word *can* to *may,* you should incorporate the change verbatim. The change is not a grammatical one; it is the essence of legal meaning. The word *can* makes an implied promise to consumers; the term *may* does not and, therefore, reduces the sponsor's potential liability in a lawsuit.

Basic Rule 33
Always try to incorporate within-scope changes.

In other instances, you can adopt the essence of the change but alter the wording. For example, a programmer suggests that you add a step to a procedure and suggests the exact wording. The programmer writes the step in third person, passive voice. You can rewrite it in the second person, active voice. Use your best judgment for determining when to follow a change verbatim and when you can improvise.

Within-scope changes also include those that result from enhanced understanding of the technical material. Designing and developing a course is much like peeling away the layers of an onion. The further you progress in the process, the more you know. As you reach the later drafts of the process, you may experience "aha!" moments when your understanding deepens, and you want to reflect that in the course materials. During the later drafts, the "ahas" usually pertain to small points and, as a result, you modify discussions by adding short passages, a word here, a sentence there.

Within-scope changes may also enhance the quality of the presentation. As you go through the process of revision, you become increasingly aware of the manner in which you present information and you focus more on the details of presentation. You will become more aware of opportunities to make similar sections more parallel (that is, structure and presenting similar concepts in similar ways), strengthen the wording of various passages, and present information graphically. If these changes affect small passages (as long as a section) and as long as making these changes will not affect your original estimates of the budget and schedule, make these changes.

For example, as you prepare the second draft, you notice that a text passage could easily be replaced by a visual. You prepare the visual yourself using graphics software installed on your computer, and you distribute the draft on schedule. In that instance, the change would be within scope. But suppose that you are preparing the final draft. You see a similar opportunity to replace a text passage with a visual that will likely be more effective. You need the assistance of a graphic artist to prepare the visual, but you have already spent the funds allotted for graphics. In such an instance, you should save the change for a future edition of the training program.

Basic Rule 34

The decision of whether or not a change is appropriate ultimately is a business decision.

Outside-of-Scope Changes. In the previous example, when a change to the graphics was deferred because the graphics budget had been exhausted, one might wonder about the quality of the content and how a course designer and developer could let an opportunity like this slip by. Consider this: As you prepare a final draft, reviewers will not be reviewing the course again. To make sure that the sponsor and the reviewers agree with the change, you will have to schedule a special review with them. That adds time to the process. (And, because time is money, it also raises the cost of the project.)

You have already spent your graphics budget, which means that you need additional funds to produce the unplanned-for visual. That visual will push you over the budget, and the sponsor may feel that business needs do not warrant the additional expense. Because you must meet both a schedule and budget, the additional change might improve the quality of the content but at the expense of the quality of the management of the project.

This example of a change is called an *outside-of-scope change*. Making such a change would result in an unplanned deadline extension, cost increase, or both. Following are some examples of outside-of-scope changes:

▶ significant changes to the technical information resulting from substantial changes given to you by the SMEs and that contradicts material provided earlier

▶ substantial changes to the presentation of information, such as wholesale reorganizations of the training program that were not discussed and approved during one of the review meetings or substantial changes to several sections of the course.

These changes are outside-of-scope because they are not part of the original commitments that you made. They could likely result in a delay in producing the training program and, perhaps, an increase in its total cost. The manner in which you manage these changes could ultimately affect your relationship with the sponsor; in fact, management of changes is often the pivotal element of sponsor–course designer and developer relationships. By carefully handling outside-of-scope changes, you can increase the likelihood that the relationship with the sponsor will remain intact and, at the same time, the change will be responsibly handled. Table 9-1 shows some examples of how to manage the issues that arise from out-of-scope changes.

Table 9-1. Dealing with outside-of-scope changes.

Who Initiated the Change?	How to Handle the Change
Sponsor	Inform the sponsor that the changes are outside the scope of the project and that you will be happy to make the change, but you'll need to renegotiate the schedule and the budget.
	Although you might feel a moment of trepidation before renegotiating the schedule and budget, and though your colleague might bristle at first when you raise the issue, do it anyway. Both of you will get past it and, in the long run, you stand a better chance of retaining the close relationship by asserting your needs now.
	Once you have made the commitment to incorporate the requested change and determined how the schedule and budget might be adjusted to accommodate it, formally document the change in a memo and report it in the status report so that all involved with the project are informed.
You	Changes that you initiated often seem good on the surface, but consider the full impact of the change before pursuing it. Consider the following.
	• The impact on the rest of the course in terms of other changes that may be necessary (a cascading effect, such as a change in terminology that must be corrected in every unit of the course) and how much time may be needed to make changes to those parts.
	• Whether the reviewers have adequate time to review the change: The later in the process (draft three or final draft), the less likely the reviewers have time for the change.
	• The resources needed to produce the change. If additional graphics work is needed, for example, consider whether the graphic artist has time to produce the requested visual.
	• The ultimate benefit to the learner.
	• The ultimate benefit to the sponsor. If the ultimate benefit is low, then the change might not be appropriate.
	If, after considering these issues, you still feel that the change is appropriate, request the sponsor's support before actually making the change.

Getting It Done

As part of the process of designing and developing course materials, you conduct formative evaluation—that is, assessment of the effectiveness of training programs while they are still under development. Course designers and developers typically conduct three types of reviews: technical reviews, through which SMEs assess the accuracy of the content; pilot tests, in which the training program is presented for a trial run, its effectiveness assessed, and suggestions for improvement noted; and production reviews, which primarily consist of editing, in which someone acts as the first learner of a training program and identifies inconsistencies, grammatical problems, and similar challenges.

Use exercise 9-1 to guide you through the process of scheduling and coordinating reviews. It tells you which reviews you should schedule at each of the three major drafts and presents issues to consider when you go through the reviews. This chart also suggests ways to manage within-scope and out-of-scope changes.

Exercise 9-1. Evaluating your learning program.

Types of Formative Evaluation

At This Draft:	Conduct These Types of Evaluations:
First	☐ Technical review Name the reviewers and their roles:_____ When review drafts will be sent: _____ When review drafts will be returned: _____ ☐ Editorial review (optional) Name the editor: _____ When review drafts will be sent: _____ When review drafts will be returned: _____
Second	☐ Technical review Name the reviewers and their roles: _____ When review drafts will be sent: _____ When review drafts will be returned: _____ ☐ Editorial review (optional) Name the editor: _____ When review drafts will be sent: _____ When review drafts will be returned: _____

(continued on page 176)

Exercise 9-1. Evaluating your learning program (continued).

At This Draft:	Conduct These Types of Evaluations:
Second (continued)	☐ Pilot test (also called pilot class) Name the participants: _____ Special requirements for the class facility: _____ _____ When the class is scheduled: _____ Name the facilitator for comments (if using one): _____ Name the instructor (if someone other than you): _____
Third	☐ Technical review (if needed) Name the reviewers and their roles:_____ _____ When review drafts will be sent: _____ When review drafts will be returned: _____ ☐ Editorial review (optional) Name the editor: _____ When review drafts will be sent: _____ When review drafts will be returned: _____
Final	☐ Editorial review Name the editor: _____ When review drafts will be sent: _____ When review drafts will be returned: _____

This chapter concludes the discussion of designing and developing courses. Chapter 10 describes how to administer, market, and support a training program once you are ready for learners to take it.

The Basics of Administering Your Course

What's Inside This Chapter

This chapter introduces you to the basics of administering, marketing, and supporting a training program. Specifically this chapter addresses the following:

▶ The basics of administering training programs, including classroom coordination, enrollment, and follow-up
▶ The basics of marketing training programs, such as the "must have" marketing information and "must consider" issues of scheduling (as it relates to marketing a course)
▶ The basics of supporting training programs, including providing services to learners, scheduling maintenance to the technical content, managing the evaluation of the program
▶ The basics of closing the course design and development project.

In addition, a worksheet at the end of this chapter identifies what you need to administer, market, and support a training program.

As a course designer and developer, you spend the bulk of your time and energies designing and developing the training program. But, the success of your efforts significantly depends on what happens after the training program is complete—how the program is administered, marketed, and supported. Although course designers and developers often do not play a central role in these activities, your planning for them as you design and develop the training program and your oversight of them after the program is in use goes a long way in ensuring that your training program has the impact that you intended.

Basic Rule 35

The success of your training program depends on the administration, marketing, and support of your program. What makes these tasks challenging is that others handle some or all of these tasks.

This chapter provides you with an overview of administration issues from the perspective of a course designer and developer. It begins by providing an overview of administrative activities. Next, this chapter explains how to market a training program. Last, the chapter explains how to support a training program by addressing many of the human and technical issues that arise when learners take courses.

The Basics of Administering Courses

Administering a training program refers to those activities involved in running classroom courses and distributing workbook-based courses. More specifically, administering a training program involves scheduling classes, enrolling learners and confirming their registration, preparing for learning sessions, closing a class, and providing follow-up reports. The following sections discuss these activities.

Basic Rule 36

To make sure that your training program runs as planned, oversee its scheduling, enrollment processes, and administration of the classroom, even if you do not plan to teach the course.

Scheduling Classes

One of the key factors in the success of a course is scheduling. Scheduling is a tricky issue—an effective choice can result in success that beats expectations, but ineffective choices can result in courses that fail to meet expectations.

Scheduling classes involves—for classroom courses—reserving classroom space for that course (and other facilities, if needed) and arranging for an instructor to teach the class session. For example, suppose that you are administering a training program for new managers. If demand is high, you might schedule classes once a month. For each class session, you must reserve a classroom and make sure that an instructor is available to present the material.

For workbook-based courses, courses are usually available whenever the learner wants to take them. In some organizations, however, learners take self-study courses in a learning center (a facility where people can take courses at their own pace; the environment is conducive to learning; and where there is easy access to equipment, books, tutors, and other resources needed in the course).

Similarly, you might prefer to limit the number of learners in a class. In such instances, you might make sure that the classroom holds just the desired number of people—no more, no less.

There are some additional issues to consider as you schedule a course:

▸ Schedule classes where your learners are located. One of the challenges of scheduling is figuring out where to schedule classes. If you have effectively targeted the learning population, you can determine where they are physically located. Schedule the classes in a location convenient for the majority of

Noted

As the course designer and developer, your primary interest in scheduling is making sure that your class is scheduled at optimum times and that the administrators have reserved the classrooms best suited to your course. For example, you might require that learners have access to computers during the class session. In such instances, you want to make sure that your class is reserved in a computer lab, a room with many computers (usually at least one computer for every two learners).

learners. For example, if you are scheduling product training classes for your customers, and 30 percent of your customers live in San Francisco and 20 percent live in Boston, then approximately 30 percent of your class sessions should take place in San Francisco and 20 percent in Boston.

▶ If you are scheduling a required course (one that each intended learner must take), try to schedule as many class sessions as early as possible, so learners do not have to wait for a class session.

▶ Avoid scheduling classes near holidays. Generally, classes scheduled the same weeks as national holidays tend to draw poorly. Even when attendance is required, learners' attention might be on vacation even if their bodies show up in the classroom.

▶ For classes scheduled in the evening, try to avoid Friday evening. That is considered part of the weekend. Even if learners are attending a class for professional development, they generally prefer to do so on weeknights.

▶ Also, try to avoid scheduling classes on religious and cultural holidays, even if they affect a relatively small number of learners in your organization. Scheduling on these dates creates an unnecessary dilemma for some learners and may be interpreted as insensitivity.

Enrolling Learners and Confirming Their Registration

Enrollment is an activity in which participants reserve seats in a classroom course or start a workbook. After a learner enrolls in a course, the course administrator (usually someone other than the course designer and developer) often sends a confirmation to the learner and, just before class starts (up to a week in advance), the administrator sends a reminder that the learner is scheduled to attend the course.

Both the confirmation and reminder letters state the name of the class session, a course number (if the organization uses them), the date and time of the class, and the name of the instructor. The confirmation also reminds the learner about charges (if any) and provides the name of an administrator to contact with questions. Figure 10-1 is an example of a confirmation letter. A reminder letter is just a variation on the confirmation letter.

Most organizations have documented processes for handling class enrollments, including standardized enrollment and confirmation letters.

As the course designer and developer, you have these interests in enrollment:

▶ Making sure that the enrollment process is easy to complete. The easier a time that learners have enrolling in class sessions, the more likely they are to

Figure 10-1. Example of an enrollment confirmation letter.

Dear John:

This is a note to confirm your enrollment in Sales School for New Marketing Representatives (course SS 100).

The course is scheduled:

Monday, November 17 through Friday, November 21
9:00 am to 5:00 pm
IS Classroom 5
Instructor: Steven Ip

Your department has been charged $2395.00 for this class. If you cannot attend, please let us know 2 weeks in advance or your department will be charged. If you must cancel with less than 2 weeks' notice, your department will still be charged for the class, but you may send an alternate in your place or reserve a space for yourself in a later class.

If you have questions about this course, please contact me at extension 4599 or trainingadmin@companyname.com.

Thank you for your enrollment. We look forward to seeing you in class.

Best regards,

Lucy Hyatt
Training Administrator

register for classes. Easy enrollment involves clear instructions (so that prospective learners know exactly what they need to do to enroll and which information they need to have when they do so), appropriate documentation (any information required to accurately identify the learner and get enrollment and payment information, but not so much that the learner perceives the requests as cumbersome or intrusive), quick processing of the request, and courteous handling of registration. To ensure such ease and consistency, many organizations turn to learning management systems—software that handles course enrollments and automatically sends confirmation and reminder letters.

▶ Making sure that the learners have prerequisite knowledge when enrolling for courses. If learners do not have the prerequisite knowledge, they will flounder in class. Many learning management systems can verify whether learners have taken prerequisites before letting them enroll in courses. If a person handles enrollment in your organization, you need to make sure that the enrollment coordinator checks for prerequisites.

▶ Making sure that learners receive all pre-class announcements, such as work that they should complete before class (called *prework*), a list of equipment they might need to bring to class, and similar types of announcements.

These issues also apply to enrollment in workbook courses. The primary difference is that learners usually can begin workbook courses immediately after enrolling in them.

Preparing for Learning Sessions

Preparation is an activity in which the administrator makes sure that all of the resources are available for a class session. For classroom courses, this includes:

▶ general supplies, such as markers for the white boards, paper for flip charts, name tags for learners (some organizations pre-print these, others provide blank name tags for learners to prepare), blank pads and pens, any appropriate general information about the facility (emergency numbers, locations of rest rooms, information about lunch facilities, and so forth), postclass evaluation forms (especially if the name of the course and instructor and date of the class session are pre-printed on the form), and coffee, donuts, and other catering (if provided, as many organizations do).

▶ learner's materials (often called learners' packets), which usually consist of the student guide, and other supplies that might be needed. For example, learners in an equipment maintenance course might be given a screwdriver so that they could remove the external casing of the equipment.

▶ materials for exercises. For computer-based exercises, make sure that all software and files have been installed, that passwords are set for each student and the instructor, and that each PC really works. For other exercises, make sure that any special materials are available (those not already mentioned).

▸ audiovisual supplies, such as an overhead or slide projector; video, CD, or DVD players (and monitors, if needed); and microphones (if needed).

▸ room setup, which usually refers to the arrangement of tables. Figure 10-2 shows the choices available.

Because improper preparations for courses can lead to an unpleasant class experience, you, as the course designer and developer, must pay attention to these issues. Specifically, you focus on:

▸ providing a setup list, especially in terms of general supplies

▸ providing audiovisual requirements to the administrator

▸ recommending a setup for the classroom

▸ providing a master copy of the student guide for copying and binding, as well as any unique instructions that administrators must consider as they copy and bind the materials (as discussed in chapters 7 and 8).

Think About This

The setup for a classroom usually refers to the arrangement of places for learners. Training classrooms are typically set up in one of the ways shown in figure 10-2:

- *classroom (upper left):* Rectangular tables are arranged with seats on one side, facing the instructor, usually with three or four seats per table. The tables provide surfaces on which learners can write, but group work (other than groups with two or three people) is a bit challenging.
- *rounds,* also called *workshop (upper right):* Several round tables, each with six to 10 seats, are arranged in the room. Learners can write on the tabletops. The arrangement is ideal for group work because participants face each other. However, two of the seats usually have their backs to the instructor.
- *theater (bottom left):* Individual chairs are placed next to each other in rows. This configuration allows for the largest number of seats, but, because participants have no writing surface, note-taking is difficult. Also, group work is difficult.

Figure 10-2. A variety of classroom setups.

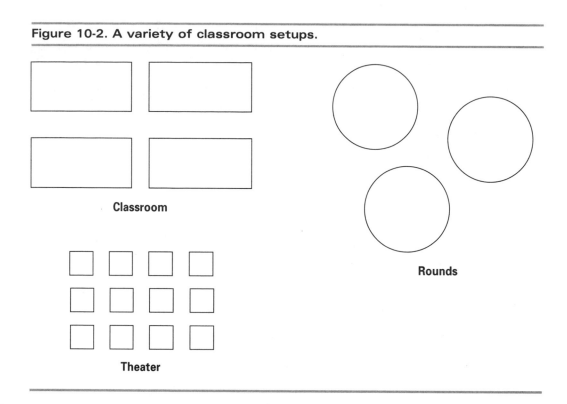

Closing a Class

Closing a class involves making sure that learners receive credit for participation and that the classroom is returned to its original state. Specifically, closing a course involves the following activities:

▸ giving credit to those learners who complete the course requirements. In some instances, anyone who attends the course receives credit for participation. In other instances, learners must have met additional requirements, such as passing a posttest.

▸ providing certificates to learners who complete the course (optional, but a popular means of recognizing learners for completing training courses). Figure 10-3 provides an example of a certificate of completion.

▸ cleaning the classroom.

▸ collecting evaluations.

As an instructor, your primary concern is making sure that the learners who complete course requirements receive the credit for completing the course.

Figure 10-3. Example of a certificate of completion.

IS Training

This certifies that

John Smith

has completed

Sales School for New Marketing Representatives (course SS 100).
Monday, November 17 – Friday, November 20

Steven Ip   *Lucy Hyatt*

Steven Ip (instructor)   Lucy Hyatt (administrator)

Providing Follow-up Reports

In many organizations, administrators perform some additional tasks after a class ends. These are called follow-up activities and include

- providing a summary of class evaluations
- providing a report of the class completions
- sending a postclass follow-up (usually a level 3 evaluation) and compiling and reporting the responses.

Course designers and developers take a special interest in these reports because they usually provide information about the number of people who attended a course, their opinions of it, and the material that "stuck" after training. Some administrators automatically distribute this information, but, in some cases, you may need to ask the administrators to do so.

The Basics of Marketing Courses

Planning announcements and promotions for new training programs is essential to their success because prospective learners do not find out about them through osmosis.

Noted

In most organizations, the course designer and developer is responsible for marketing the course, even if he or she does not have general marketing responsibilities (much less training in how to market a course).

The following sections describe marketing issues that affect course designers and developers: the must-have information to market a course and issues to consider when scheduling class sessions.

Must-Have Marketing Materials

To promote a new training program, you first prepare *collateral material* about it. As banks require a tangible guarantee called collateral before making most loans, so marketing efforts require some tangible information called collateral material before a new product can be announced and promoted. Collateral also remains available throughout the life of the course. This collateral material for a training program includes a course description (figure 10-4) to publish in a course catalog.

Other Promotional Materials

The second part of the strategy for marketing a training program involves preparing promotional material about it. Promotional material raises awareness of a course in

Basic Rule 37

Every course must have a course description for marketing purposes. A description typically contains this information:

- title of the course
- length: the number of hours (for courses less than four hours) or days
- description, 50 to 75 words that motivate readers to take the course while accurately representing the content. Begin the description with an action verb.
- objectives, the instructional objectives
- audience: descriptive information about intended learners
- prerequisites: Although these are typically stated as course titles, you provide more help to learners by stating the skills they should have mastered before starting the learning program, then state the courses that teach those skills.

Figure 10-4. Example of a course description.

25 Tips for Communicating Online
Length: 1 day

Prerequisites: Learners should be able to develop user's guides and other printed material for user support. This material is presented in Technical Communication 101.

About This Seminar: 25 Tips for Communicating Online explores how to adapt writing skills honed for the printed page to the screen. Learn how to overcome the limitations of reading online through effective organization and tight writing. Specifically, learn:

- techniques for structuring information online
- issues in screen design and navigation online
- ways to engage readers through visual variety and interaction
- tight writing techniques
- tips for bringing readers to your online content.

Through hands-on exercises, you'll practice the techniques presented in class.

Who Should Attend: Technical communicators, business communicators, and trainers who are experienced in writing for the page or developing material for the classroom and want to reorient their skills for the computer screen. Experienced online communicators and Web-based training (WBT) developers might find this workshop a good refresher (and may pick up a few new ideas, too).

What You Will Learn:

- Main Objective: Adapt strategies for presenting content from the page or classroom to the screen.

- Supporting Objectives: To achieve the objective, you should be able to:

1 Name the four fundamental ways that communicating online differs from communicating on the page or in the classroom.
2. Describe at least three ways that online content differs from content in other media.
3. Explain how to help users navigate through online content.
4. Explain how to effectively use typography online.
5. Explain how to place content on the screen to maximum effect.
6. Describe at least three techniques for communicating interactively online.
7. Describe at least three techniques for communicating visually online.
8. Describe at least three techniques for writing online material.
9. State the role of tools in producing online content.
10. Describe at least two issues to consider when maintaining online content.

the short run and is only intended to have a shelf life of four to eight weeks. Promotional material can take many forms, including:

- catch-the-eye-quickly promotions, such as flyers about the training program, posters, and banner ads on corporate Websites (including intranet sites)
- "off-the-wall" promotions, such as fortune cookies with custom-printed fortunes that all recommend your training program, cakes decorated with a message about your training program, and other edible items
- email messages that announce or promote the training program, usually sent to graduates of previous courses and people who fit the demographic profile of the intended learners.

Create a Promotional Plan

After you identify the type of material you need to promote the training program, prepare a plan for the types of promotions you will use and when. Here is a suggested timeline:

- *Before the training program is available:* Prepare collateral material and make sure that it is ready for the day you announce the training program. Also prepare some promotional materials that will raise awareness of the program. Finally, generate good advance support for the training program. One way to do so involves piloting the program with a group that is anticipated to respond positively to it. Their positive experiences will generate a good word-of-mouth, which should inspire others in the organization to consider trying the training program.
- *A month to six weeks after the training program is available:* Prepare another wave of promotional materials to maintain the awareness of the training program following its initial launch.
- *On an ongoing basis (quarterly or semiannually):* Promote the availability of the training program.
- *When enrollment drops:* Plan another round of promotion to rebuild awareness of the training program. Ongoing publication of a catalog also helps to maintain awareness.

Finally, make sure that you leave time in your schedule to perform these activities. Some organizations devote as much as 20 percent of their resources to the marketing effort. Although that might not be feasible in every organization, failing to devote more than an hour or two to promotion could doom the training program to low usage and poor results.

When should you send marketing announcements about classes? Send first announcements of class sessions 10 to 12 weeks before they are scheduled—no sooner, no later. This timeframe has been verified over years of research.

The 10- to 12-week guideline seems to work well in a wide variety of instances. Early birds might want to announce the course with more than a 12-week lead time. When learners see that, the timeframe is too far away and they tend to overlook the announcement, figuring they can come enroll later. Unfortunately, many forget about the course and never enroll.

In contrast, others might claim that because this is the age of the Internet and instant communication, people do not need as much advance notice. But most learners need to clear their schedules well in advance to make sure that they have time to attend. They need several weeks notice to do so. Similarly, many corporate learners need time to receive management approval to attend a training class (especially if they must spend external funds).

Basic Rule 38
The support that you provide to learners leaves a lasting impression about the entire learning experience.

The Basics of Supporting Training Programs

In addition to administering and marketing a course, course designers and developers must also consider how the course is supported. In some cases, support involves additional work for the course designer and developer. In other cases, the course designer and developer does not need to provide the support, but the quality of that support directly reflects on her or him anyway.

The following sections describe some of the key areas of support: services to learners, maintenance of the technical content, and evaluations.

Providing Support to Learners

Despite the best attempts to explain content clearly, some learners might not understand it. Similarly, other learners might seek enrichment or individual attention not available in the classroom. In these and similar instances, course designers and developers provide services to learners primarily through tutoring and enrichment.

Tutoring. Tutoring usually occurs outside of class—sometimes long after class is complete. It can take many forms, such as communication by email; a toll-free number where learners can call for tutoring; and office hours, which can be conducted in-person or online (chat, instant messaging, or collaboration software). Promote the availability of tutoring, which many learners and their managers perceive as a value-added service.

Regardless of the means used to provide tutoring, one challenge is clearly setting expectations. Issues that you need to address are: how quickly can a learner expect a response? How long after the course is completed do you provide tutoring services? Some for-profit providers provide tutoring for up to six months after a class.

If someone other than you will provide tutoring services, then that person must become familiar with the content of the course before its launch, and you should provide the tutor with answers to anticipated questions.

No matter who is to do the tutoring, be sure to anticipate how much time and staff you'll need for tutorial support. Otherwise, questions will seem like interruptions, and learners might be treated with less than the consideration they deserve. The actual time to set aside varies, depending on how many learners take the training program. At first, you might set aside the same amount of time that a typical college professor leaves for office hours: between two and four hours a week. As the course progresses, monitor the actual time spent to determine how much time to leave in the future.

Enrichment. Learner support through enrichment is usually provided through a Website associated with the course. The Website would have additional readings and other resources, such as specialized calculators. Sometimes, instructors limit access to these Websites through the use of passwords. Be sure to set aside adequate time and staff for maintaining the course Website.

Scheduling Maintenance to the Course Content

If you know in advance that the course content is likely to change after you develop it, you should plan for that as part of maintenance. For example, if you develop a training program about a new product and you know that new models or enhancements will be made available three to six months later, you should plan for that as part of the planning for course maintenance.

Generally, updates to the content fall into three categories:

► minor revision, which involves changes to specific passages, usually a word or sentence here and there, an occasional paragraph, and perhaps a new or changed illustration in the slides or supplemental materials

► moderate revision, which involves the addition of new sections, as well as changes to specific passages and graphics

► major revision, which involves an overhaul to the content.

Determine the extent of the revision and use that to estimate the resources needed to make it.

Managing the Evaluation of the Course

As part of the early phases of design, you developed the plan for evaluating the course. You prepared drafts of satisfaction surveys, tests, and follow-up assessments before you even decided how to format and present the content.

As you prepare for the launch and maintenance of the course you should plan to administer these evaluations, and compile and report the results. Specifically, consider the following:

► Update the evaluation instruments. Because you wrote them before developing the content and might have made adjustments to the objectives of the training program as you designed and developed it, the evaluations must reflect those changes to provide valid feedback.

► Plan for administration of the evaluations. Consider how you will solicit feedback on course satisfaction. Will you ask every student to complete a form before he or she leaves the classroom (as is typical) or will you use follow-up methods, like randomly-generated email messages and phone calls? (These might be especially helpful with workbooks; learners are less likely to respond to satisfaction surveys included in those courses.) Consider, too, how you will test for learning. Will you administer a test? How will you keep records? To whom will you report results? Consider how you will track long-term changes in behavior that result from the learning. How will you contact learners to get their input: by email, phone, or some other method? Whom else will you survey to assess whether learners are using the content taught in the training program on the job?

▶ Report the results. Specifically, consider who receives these results: members of learning team? A sponsor for whom you developed the learning program? What format will the reports take? Do different groups receive different reports? Will you compare results across courses?

Closing a Design and Development Project

The last thing you do on a course design and development project is close it. Closing the project involves two activities: conducting the postmortem and preparing a project history file.

Basic Rule 39

Provide complete records of a training project: both about the experience of developing it (through a postmortem) and a history of its progress (through a project history course) so other course designers and developers can learn from the experience.

Conducting a Postmortem

One of the most significant activities you can conduct after completing a project is one in which the development team identifies the lessons they learned from it and might carry into future projects. One of the most effective methods of identifying these lessons is a special meeting of the project team called the *postmortem*.

A postmortem is a meeting of all members of the project team, including SMEs, graphic designers, sponsors, your manager, and, of course, you. It occurs at the end of the project. Its purpose is to identify

▶ what went well and should be repeated on future projects, and

▶ what did not go well and how to avoid these situations on future projects.

It's important to ask the team what went right because by the time a project wraps up, team members are often focused on what went wrong. It's important to recall the positive aspects of the project and end on a high note. Also, while the group is discussing what to improve on future projects, don't allow the postmortem to become a "finger-pointing" session. Use the postmortem as an opportunity to identify problems and suggest solutions to them.

Noted

The postmortem should provide time for everyone on the course development team to thank one another for their contributions. Often during the course of a project, team members become so comfortable working with one another that they do not thank them for their contributions or acknowledge exceptional work. As a result, team members might not realize that their colleagues appreciate these contributions. The postmortem provides a formal opportunity for team members to offer one another such recognition.

Here are some tips for conducting a postmortem:

1. Send a meeting notice to team members at least two weeks in advance. Invite all team members to participate, including representatives from the sponsoring organization.
2. Prepare and distribute an agenda before the meeting. A typical postmortem is no longer than 90 minutes, 60 if possible. The agenda should set aside time for discussing what went well, identifying what needs to be improved for future projects, and offering acknowledgments and thanks to the team members.
3. Identify a recorder to keep the minutes and distribute them after the meeting.
4. Close the postmortem with some sort of celebration. For example, you could provide a cake that says "Congratulations" or a small gift for each team member.
5. Publish the minutes of the postmortem, ideally within two business days.
6. For those suggestions that require changes to your organization's policies and procedures, provide a follow-up memo to team members within one month of the meeting to tell them whether the policy and procedures will be changed.

At the meeting, create a positive, productive environment by emphasizing the positive and providing each team member with an opportunity to speak. For example, when you ask, "What went right?" and "What do we need to improve on future projects?" go around the room and ask each person to provide at least one suggestion.

Also avoid passing judgment on comments. As a result of their role or because of their personalities, different team members have different perceptions about the project. Some might have had a positive experience, and others not. Only by hearing how each team member perceived the project can the entire development team better understand the just-completed project.

Postmortems provide valuable closure to projects, letting participants emotionally separate from one project so they can move onto the next. Therefore, postmortem meetings are beneficial whether members of the team will work together or individually on their next projects.

Preparing a Project History File

A project history file is a repository of all key information about the development of a training project. This information can be used in a number of different ways:

- ▶ Records of the time and cost of each completed activity can be used as tools to estimate the schedule and budget of future projects; the more you base future estimates on past performance, the more accurate they are likely to become.
- ▶ Records of proposals and needs analyses can be used as input to future projects. In some cases, the information can be re-used as is and can reduce the time needed to conduct an analysis. In others, it serves as one of many sources of input for the project.
- ▶ Design plans can be reused or serve as a framework for building designs of new courses (much like architects base designs for future outlets of franchised fast-food restaurants on previous ones).
- ▶ Lessons learned can be used to improve the overall management of a project.

Although each organization needs different information in a project file, some common elements include

- ▶ project proposal
- ▶ report of the needs analysis
- ▶ design plans

- prototypes
- copies of each draft
- feedback from any tests of pilot tests
- copies of comments submitted for each plan and draft
- copies of the planned and actual budgets and schedules
- at least two hard copies and backup electronic copies of all finished course materials and accompanying materials
- minutes of the postmortem meeting and other "lessons learned"
- names of contact people.

Save the history file in a secure place. If your company has an offsite archive, the paper version of the history file might be stored there, in addition to maintaining a copy at your location. Many organizations also maintain electronic copies of the history file.

Getting It Done

After completing the design and development of a training program, your responsibilities continue. Specifically, you should oversee administration, marketing, and support of the training program to make sure that it works as well in practice as you had hoped it would in design.

Administration involves scheduling, enrollment, and classroom coordination. Marketing involves preparing collateral (must-have) material as well as related promotions and a marketing strategy. Support involves providing services to learners, scheduling maintenance to the technical content, and managing the evaluation of the program. Last is closing the project with a postmortem meeting and a project history file.

Use exercise 10-1 to guide you through the process of administering, marketing, and supporting a training program.

This chapter concludes the discussion of how to design and develop a training process. This book has taken you through the ADDIE process. After providing you with some background principles in chapter 1 and guidance for starting a project in chapter 2, this book walked you through the analysis phases (chapters 3 and 4), design phases (chapters 5 and 6), development phases (chapters 7, 8, and 9), and implementation and evaluation phases (chapter 10).

Exercise 10-1. Administering your course.

Preparing for Learning Sessions	☐ General supplies
	☐ Learners' materials
	   ___ Special materials for exercises
	   ___ Audiovisual equipment
	   ___ Room setup
	☐ Closing a class
	   ___ Processing completions
	   ___ Providing completion certificates
	   ___ Cleaning the classroom
	   ___ Processing evaluations
	☐ Providing follow-up reports on attendance and evaluation

Marketing the Course	☐ Prepare a course description
	☐ Prepare a promotional plan that promotes the course at these times:
	   ___ Upon announcement
	   ___ Within a month or so of announcement
	   ___ Ongoing marketing
	   ___ When enrollment drops

Scheduling the Course	☐ Announce class session eight to 12 weeks in advance ☐ Avoid vacation times ☐ Avoid religious and other holidays
Providing Support to Learners	☐ Tutoring ☐ Enrichment

Closing a Project	☐ Conduct a postmortem
	☐ Prepare a project history file with two copies of these:
	   ___ Project proposal
	   ___ Report of the needs analysis
	   ___ Design plans
	   ___ Prototypes
	   ___ Copies of each draft
	   ___ Feedback from any tests of pilot tests
	   ___ Copies of comments submitted for each plan and draft
	   ___ Copies of the planned and actual budgets and schedules

References

Brusaw, C., G. Alred, and W. Oliu. (2000). *Handbook of Technical Writing.* New York: St. Martin's Press.

Carliner, S. (2002). *Designing E-Learning.* Alexandria, VA: ASTD.

Carliner, S. (1995). The Eight Secrets of Starting a Successful Work Team. *Performance & Instruction, 24*(2).

Gagne, R.M. (1985). *The Conditions of Learning and Theory of Instruction,* 4th edition. New York: Holt, Rinehart, and Winston.

Hackos, J.T. (1994). *Managing Your Documentation Projects.* New York: John Wiley & Sons.

Kirkpatrick, D.L. (1998). *Evaluating Training Programs: The Four Levels,* 2d edition. San Francisco: Berrett-Koehler.

Knowles, M. (1988). *The Modern Practice of Adult Education: From Pedagogy to Andragogy.* Cambridge, MA: Cambridge Book Co.

Mager, R. (1997). *Preparing Instructional Objectives.* Atlanta: Center for Effective Performance.

Robinson, D., and J. Robinson. (1989). *Training for Impact.* San Francisco: Jossey-Bass.

Wurman, R.S. (1989). *Information Anxiety: What to Do When Information Doesn't Tell You What You Need to Know.* New York: Doubleday.

Additional Resources

Chapter 1
To learn more about:

- **The example with customer service representatives,** read Dana and James Robinson's *Training for Impact.* (1989). San Francisco: Jossey-Bass.

- **Human performance improvement,** read Harold Stolovich's and Erica Keeps's *Handbook of Human Performance Improvement.* (1999). San Francisco: Jossey-Bass.

- **Andragogy,** read Malcolm Knowles's *The Modern Practice of Adult Education: Andragogy Versus Pedagogy,* revised edition. (1988). Englewood Cliffs, NJ: Cambridge Book Company.

Chapter 2
To learn more about:

- **The instructional systems design process in general,** read Walter Dick's and Lou Carey's *The Systematic Design of Instruction,* 5th edition. Upper Saddle River, NJ: Pearson Addison Wesley.

- **Project management,** read Karen Overfield's *Developing and Managing Organizational Learning: A Guide to Effective Training Project Management.* Alexandria, VA: ASTD.

Chapter 3
To learn more about:

- **Needs analysis in general,** read Allison Rossett's *First Things Fast: A Handbook for Performance Analysis.* (1998). San Francisco: Jossey Bass/Pfeiffer.

▶ **Clarifying the goals of an instructional program,** read Robert Mager's *Goal Analysis.* (1997). Atlanta: Center for Effective Performance.

Chapter 4

To learn more about:

▶ **Writing instructional objectives,** read Robert Mager's *Preparing Instructional Objectives.* (1997). Atlanta: Center for Effective Performance.

▶ **Writing tests,** read Robert Mager's *Measuring Instructional Results.* (1997). Atlanta: Center for Effective Performance.

▶ **Evaluating training programs,** read either Donald Kirkpatrick's *Evaluating Training Programs: The Four Levels,* 2d edition. (1998). San Francisco: Berrett-Koehler; or Richard Swanson's and Elwood Holton's *Results: How to Assess Performance, Learning, and Perceptions in Organizations.* (1999). San Francisco: Berrett-Koehler.

Chapter 5

To learn more about:

▶ **Designing courses for e-learning** (which this book doesn't discuss much), check out Saul Carliner's *Designing E-Learning.* (2002). Alexandria, VA: ASTD.

▶ **Information overload and the structure of information,** read Richard Saul Wurman's *Information Anxiety 2001: What to Do When Information Doesn't Tell You What You Need to Know.* (2001). New York: Doubleday.

Chapter 8

To learn more about:

▶ **Clearly writing material,** read William Strunk Jr.'s and E.B. White's *The Elements of Style,* 4th edition. (2000). Upper Saddle River, NJ: Pearson Allyn & Bacon.

▶ **Designing pages,** read Robin Williams's and John Tollett's *The Non-Designer's Web Book: An Easy Guide to Creating, Designing, and Posting Your Own Web Site.* (1994). Berkeley, CA: Peachpit Press.

Chapter 9

To learn more about:

▶ **Editing,** read Karen Judd's *Copyediting, A Practical Guide,* 3d edition. (2001). Menlo Park, CA: Crisp Publications; or Marjorie Skillin's and Robert Malcolm Gay's classic, *Words Into Type.* (1974). Upper Saddle River, NJ: Pearson.

Chapter 10

To learn more about:

▶ **Training administration and marketing,** read Jean Barbazette's *The Trainer's Support Handbook: A Guide to Managing the Administrative Details of Training.* (2001). New York: McGraw-Hill.

About the Author

■ ■

Saul Carliner is an assistant professor of educational technology at Concordia University in Montreal, where he teaches courses in human performance technology, knowledge management, and qualitative research. His research interests include emerging genres of online communication and means of assessing the effectiveness of content for the workplace. He has also served on the faculties of the City University of Hong Kong, University of Minnesota, and Bentley College.

Also an industry consultant, Carliner advises corporations on strategic issues in e-learning and communication. His clients include Berlitz, Guidant, IBM, Microsoft, ST Microelectronics, 3M, VNU Business Media, and several government agencies. His other books include *Designing E-Learning* (ASTD, 2002), *An Overview of Online Learning* (HRD Press, 1999), and, with Carol Barnum, *Techniques for Technical Communicators* (Macmillan, 1992). Carliner is also a popular workshop presenter. His training workshops have been presented at the following events: TRAINING, Online Learning, ISPI conferences, and ASTD Webinars.

He is a fellow and past international president of the Society for Technical Communication, past president of the Atlanta chapter of the International Society for Performance Improvement, and holds a Ph.D. in instructional technology from Georgia State University.